WORLD OF BASEBALL

Speed

Steve Fiffer

A REDEFINITION BOOK

Speed

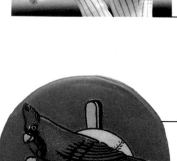

Speed in baseball is elusive, both as a commodity and as a statistic. It's the first thing scouts look for in a ballplayer, because it's the one thing that can't be taught. Yet it is the least measurable weapon in the game. Timing and rhythm are baseball's moorings; speed can knock both for a loop.

The Artful Dodger

**W**eather forecasters had erred in predicting rain for the September 23, 1962, game between the Los Angeles Dodgers and the St. Louis Cardinals. Nevertheless, the playing field at St. Louis' Sportsman's Park, particularly around first base, was wet. Maury Wills, the Dodgers' leadoff batter, was not surprised. The 29-year-old shortstop knew that when the heavens didn't cooperate, opposing teams were not above watering down the field to prevent him from getting a quick start to second base. Such tactics had done little to upset Wills. For the past several weeks, he had been speeding toward Ty Cobb's record of 96 stolen bases in a season: a mark that had stood since 1915—a full 13 years longer than Babe Ruth's home run mark lasted. Wills entered the game with a remarkable 95 steals.

With the introduction of the lively ball and the rise in home runs shortly after World War I, the stolen base lost the importance it had had during the dead-ball era. In over 40 years, no one had surpassed the 63 bases stolen by the Washington Senators' Sam Rice in 1920. Wills, himself, now in his fourth year in the major leagues, had never stolen more than 50 bases in a season; he had led the National League in 1961 with a mere 35 steals.

Wills particularly wanted to break Cobb's record that September day; it was the Dodgers' 156th game of a 162-game season. Cobb had played a 154-game schedule, but because his 1915 Detroit Tigers had been involved in two ties, he had actually set his record in the 156th game. When Wills read in

Dodger base-stealing wizard Maury Wills was famous for his fall-away hook slide, but in Game 2 of the 1963 World Series he went in headfirst (opposite) against Yankee infielders Bobby Richardson (1) and Tony Kubek for his only steal in a Dodger sweep.

Maury Wills kicked up a lot of dust in Game 3 of the 1962 NL playoff between the Dodgers and Giants with his 102nd, 103rd and 104th steals of the season. Wills stole third (above) in the seventh to help raise the Dodger lead to 4–2, but the Giants left L.A. in the dust with four in the ninth and walked off with the pennant.

the morning paper that Curt Simmons would be pitching for the Cardinals, Wills was confident: "I could steal off Curt Simmons running backwards," the outspoken shortstop later said. Simmons always took a step back before throwing to first, making him easy to read.

But shortly before the game, the Cardinals announced that Simmons had hurt his arm and would be replaced by Larry Jackson. Wills was not happy. Jackson had a good slider, and Wills had never hit well against him. Jackson also had a questionable pickoff move—some thought it amounted to a balk—that was rough on baserunners. As Wills dug in at home plate to lead off the game, he lobbied umpire Augie Donatelli, trying to persuade him that Jackson's move was illegal.

"Play ball," said Donatelli. Jackson's first pitch was a called strike and drew the wrath of the entire ballpark. The fans—Cardinal and Dodger fans alike—wanted to see him get on base and steal. It didn't take long. In the third inning, Wills singled, then stole second base as catcher Carl Sawatski's throw to shortstop Dal Maxvill missed the mark. He had tied Cobb's record.

By the seventh inning, the Dodgers trailed, 11–2. Many managers are reluctant to signal for the steal when their team needs so many runs to get back in a ballgame. But when Wills left the dugout for the on-deck circle, Dodger skipper Walter Alston told him to forget the score and go for the record if he got on base. After working the count to three and two, Wills swung at Jackson's next pitch and made contact. The ball rolled between second baseman Julian Javier and first baseman Bill White into right field for a base hit. The stadium shook with excitement, and both the Dodger and the Cardinal benches emptied, the players moving to the top steps of their dugouts.

While the crowds loved Wills, many umpires were less than thrilled by his combative attitude. According to umpire Stan Landes, whom Wills once called "blubbergut," Wills "thought he was something special and wanted the umpires to treat him as such."

The next batter, Jim Gilliam, might as well have stayed in the dugout. Jackson completely ignored him, throwing to first baseman White several times to keep Wills close to the bag. Sizing up the situation, Wills decided to try a delayed steal. "My lead was no more than five feet," he remembers. "Jackson figured that I wasn't going, the catcher and infielders relaxed momentarily, and he went into his stretch and fired to the plate.

"While the ball was in flight, I took two short steps and ran like a thief. By the time they realized I was stealing, I was halfway down the basepath. Thirty feet from second base I left the ground and dove headfirst. I was about ten feet short, and I crawled the rest of the way. The throw bounced five feet in front of second base and rolled past it.

"I remember lying on the ground with that bag in my hand for about thirty seconds. 'This is mine,' I kept saying to myself, 'and I earned it.' "

Before the season ended a week later, Wills had stolen seven more bases, bringing his season total to 104; he was thrown out only 13 times. The Dodgers lost the playoff series for the National League pennant to the San Francisco Giants, but Wills' record-shattering performance earned him recognition as the National League's Most Valuable Player.

Opposing managers and players tried any number of tricks to keep Maury Wills from stealing bases, and the Cardinals were not the only team to change the infield topography. Alvin Dark, managing the San Francisco Giants in the 1960s, earned the nickname "Swamp Fox" by telling the Candlestick Park grounds crew to water the field—and keep watering it.

Joe Torre, the Braves' first baseman, tried a different approach. When a Braves pitcher attempted to pick Wills off, Torre flopped down in front of

Continued on page 12

6' 2" 195 lbs.
BR TR

b 3/21/1939

TOMMY DAVIS
Outfield

While Maury Wills was stealing his way into the record books in 1962, Tommy Davis was pulverizing NL pitching.

The 23-year-old left fielder and third baseman led the NL with a .346 average, 230 hits and 153 RBI. His RBI total—the seventh highest in NL history—has not been topped since. He also had 27 homers and 120 runs scored, and he was magic in the clutch. "Every time there was a man on base he'd knock him in," said Dodger pitcher Sandy Koufax, "and every time there were two men on base, he'd hit a double and knock them both in."

Becoming a Dodger was the realization of a childhood dream for Davis—he just did it on the wrong coast. The best athlete at Brooklyn Boys' High, Davis signed with the Dodgers in 1956. A year later the team announced it was moving west. "My big dream was gone," he said. But his talent stayed, and Davis beat a quick path to the majors. He won his second batting title in 1963, then hit .400 in the Dodgers' World Series sweep over the Yankees.

Davis broke his ankle in 1965 and played just 17 games that year. Although he hit .313 for the Dodgers in 1966, he never regained his speed. Davis played for eight teams in the last nine years of his career. His clutch hitting helped Oakland win the AL West in 1971—he hit .464 as a pinch hitter—and Baltimore win the AL East in 1973 and 1974. "He's a *much* better hitter with men on," said Dodger manager Walt Alston. "You can't give a hitter a finer compliment than that."

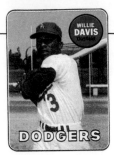

Willie Davis

The scouting report was a whiff: "He can't hit, he can't hit with power, and he can't throw." But Willie Davis could run, and he could catch, and he could do both so well that Dodger scout Ken Myers decided he could teach the young speedster the rest. What Myers discovered at Roosevelt High School in Los Angeles was a brilliant athlete, one who ran a 9.5 hundred, set an All-City high school long jump record at 25 feet, 5 inches, and once scored 36 points for the school's basketball team.

Myers converted Davis—a right-handed-hitting first baseman in high school—into a left-handed-hitting outfielder to take advantage of his speed. He also cured Davis of his sidearm delivery by making him practice throwing while lying on his back. The tutoring paid quick dividends. Davis signed with the Dodgers in 1958, and at 19 he hit .365 to win the batting title in the California League. He followed that up with another batting title, led the Pacific Coast League in runs scored, hits, triples and stolen bases, and was named *The Sporting News* Minor League Player of the Year. He had "can't miss" written all over him.

But after Davis reached the majors in 1960, he never developed into an all-around, Willie Mays-variety star. He had a fine 18-year career, including three straight .300 seasons from 1969 to 1971. His speed unnerved opponents, and at times he seemed on the brink of superstardom, as in 1969, when he put together a 31-game hitting streak, or in 1971, when he went into mid-July hitting over .350. But he struck out too much, and pitchers took advantage of his free-swinging style. "If the President throws out the first ball," one sportswriter wrote, "Willie will swing at it." Early in his career he fancied himself a power hitter, refused to bunt and as a result rarely got to use his speed, which left Dodger manager Walter Alston scratching his head. "It's crazy, because any time Willie hits a fly ball it takes away his biggest asset—speed." And although he was acknowledged as the fastest player in the game—one who could score from second on a sacrifice fly and go from first to third on a bunt—he never led the league in stolen bases.

What may have prevented Davis from realizing his potential was the happy-go-lucky attitude that made him so popular with fans, players and the press. Handsome, charming and self-assured, Davis just didn't seem to *need* baseball. "If he has a fault it's his nonchalance," said slugger Richie Allen, who joined the Dodgers in 1971. "He has a good temperament for baseball. But sometimes I think he'd be better off if he'd get more bothered by things, extend himself."

But his ability to keep the game in perspective came in handy after Game 2 of the 1966 World Series, a game in which Davis committed three errors—in one inning. In the fifth inning of a scoreless duel between Sandy Koufax and the Orioles' Jim Palmer, Davis dropped two fly balls, then made a throwing error after his second muff. His errors led to three unearned runs and a 6–0 Oriole win. Davis steadfastly maintained that he lost both balls in the sun, but the press and fans were merciless. "The balls definitely hit Willie's glove," wrote one pundit. "You could hear them clank." But Davis just wasn't the type to brood. He played the game with vitality and daring, and when the game was over, he left it on the field. Asked once why he never got rattled in pressure games, Davis replied, "It's not my life, it's not my wife, so why worry?"

Willie Davis was among the fastest—and most aggressive—baserunners of his time. "When Willie is in motion, there is only one way to hold him on third," said Dodger manager Walter Alston. "The instant he rounds second, you give him the slide sign."

WILLIE DAVIS

Outfield
Los Angeles Dodgers 1960–1973
Montreal Expos 1974
Texas Rangers 1975
St. Louis Cardinals 1975
San Diego Padres 1976
California Angels 1979

GAMES	**2,429**
AT-BATS	**9,174**
BATTING AVERAGE	
Career	**.279**
Season High	**.311**
SLUGGING AVERAGE	
Career	**.412**
Season High	**.456**
HITS	
Career	**2,561**
Season High	**198**
DOUBLES	
Career	**395**
Season High	**33**
TRIPLES	
Career	**138**
Season High	**16**
HOME RUNS	
Career	**182**
Season High	**21**
RUNS BATTED IN	
Career	**1,053**
Season High	**93**
RUNS	
Career	**1,217**
Season High	**103**
STOLEN BASES	
Career	**398**
Season High	**42**
WORLD SERIES	**1963, 1965, 1966**

Daring Duos

Having one great base-stealer is a major asset, but a second good base-stealer can take pressure off the number-one man and put additional pressure on the opponent. Maury Wills and Willie Davis combined for 136 stolen bases for the 1962 Dodgers, but that ranks them just ninth on the list of the top ten all-time base-stealing tandems with at least 30 steals each.

Team	Year	Player	SB	CS	SB%	% of team steals
Cardinals	1985	V. Coleman	110	25	.815	35.0
		W. McGee	56	16	.778	17.8
		Total	166	41	.802	52.9
Expos	1980	R. LeFlore	97	19	.836	40.9
		R. Scott	63	13	.829	26.6
		Total	160	32	.833	67.5
Cardinals	1987	V. Coleman	109	22	.832	44.0
		O. Smith	43	9	.827	17.3
		Total	152	31	.831	61.3
Cardinals	1974	L. Brock	118	33	.781	68.6
		B. McBride	30	11	.732	17.4
		Total	148	44	.771	86.0
Athletics	1983	R. Henderson	108	19	.850	46.0
		M. Davis	32	15	.681	13.6
		Total	140	34	.805	59.6

Team	Year	Player	SB	CS	SB%	% of team steals
Cardinals	1986	V. Coleman	107	14	.884	40.8
		O. Smith	31	7	.816	11.8
		Total	138	21	.868	52.7
Cardinals	1988	V. Coleman	81	27	.750	34.6
		O. Smith	57	9	.864	24.4
		Total	138	36	.793	59.0
Senators	1913	C. Milan	75	–	–	26.1
		D. Moeller	62	–	–	21.6
		Total	137	–	–	47.7
Dodgers	1962	M. Wills	104	13	.889	52.5
		W. Davis	32	7	.821	16.2
		Total	136	20	.872	68.7
Expos	1991	M. Grissom	76	17	.817	34.1
		D. DeShields	56	23	.709	25.1
		Total	132	40	.762	59.2

Official records of **Caught Stealing** for most players were not kept until 1920.

the bag while the ball was on its way. The first time this happened, Wills was blocked and tagged out, despite diving headfirst back to the bag. Wills argued with Stan Landes, the first-base umpire, claiming that Torre's move should be ruled interference—that only catchers could block a base. Landes disagreed.

The next day, Wills took matters into his own hands. He filed an edge on his spikes. Once on first, Wills took a substantial lead and drew a pickoff throw. Torre had gone down on one knee to block the base, but when he saw Wills coming, spikes first, he jumped out of the way. Wills made it back safely, but the bag itself was torn apart, leaving the stuffing hanging out. "Torre didn't say a word," Wills recalled. "He nodded at me as though the message were plain. We had an umpire who didn't know how to enforce a rule."

Later in the game, with the 5′ 11″, 170-pound Dodger speedster again at first, the pitcher tried at least five pickoff throws. On the last one, Torre blocked the base again, and Wills' spikes tore into his knee. Torre limped to the Milwaukee dugout and returned with his knee taped and blood all over his uniform. As Wills later recalled, "Joe Torre is a big hairy bull of a man, and I was afraid he would pinch my ear off. But Joe didn't even nod. . . . I assumed he knew that whenever a baseman blocks the path, he's vulnerable, and he accepted that. . . . But Joe was not one to forget. When he was playing catcher and I was running into home, he would make me eat dirt. Torre wouldn't just tag me with the ball; he tried to pound me into the ground with it. All part of the game of stopping the stealer."

Maury Wills did more than sound the death knell to Ty Cobb's long-standing individual record; he rang in a new era in which speed became as important to the game as it had been at the end of the 19th century.

Even though the color barrier in baseball had been broken in 1947, the 1960s saw the first large-scale recruitment of black and Hispanic players—who had been raised on the running game—into the major leagues. Naturally, their presence changed the style of play in the majors. Two other changes also made speed a more prominent part of the game: an expanded strike zone made hits harder to come by and stealing bases a better risk, and the introduction of artificial turf in ballparks like the Houston Astrodome and Busch Stadium in St. Louis rewarded quickness. The teams with speed on the bases and in the field were poised at the starter's block, ready to assume prominence.

In 1958 the National League champion Milwaukee Braves stole only 26 bases the entire season, while the Dodgers led the league with 73 steals. When the Dodgers won the pennant in 1963, the year after Wills' record-breaking season, they led the league with 124 steals. Ten years later, three of the four division winners—Cincinnati, Baltimore and world champion Oakland—led their divisions in steals. The A's and the Reds, the dominant teams of the 1970s, were annually among the leaders in stolen bases, Oakland setting an American League record with 341 stolen bases in 1976. That same year, the 24 major league teams combined for more than 3,000 steals, quadrupling the total compiled by 16 teams 20 years earlier in 1956.

In the 1980s St. Louis Cardinals manager Whitey Herzog developed a lineup full of speedsters by signing Ozzie Smith, Willie McGee and Vince Coleman. Oakland's rising star, Jose Canseco, became a new kind of superhero, a player capable of hitting 40 home runs and stealing as many bases.

Although not known for his fielding, Wills (above, with Cincinnati's Art Shamsky) won Gold Gloves in 1961 and 1962, and in 1965 led NL shortstops with 535 assists.

Maury Wills scored 130 runs in 1962, and more often than not it was Tommy Davis (above, sliding) who drove him in. Davis won two-thirds of the Triple Crown that season with 153 RBI and a .346 average. He also managed to steal 18 bases, third on the team behind Wills and Willie Davis.

With renewed emphasis on running, Wills' record lasted only a dozen years until the Cardinals' Lou Brock stole 118 bases in 1974. Brock eventually broke Cobb's career mark of 892 steals, but his own single-season milestone survived only until 1982, when Oakland's Rickey Henderson—who was only four years old when Wills passed Cobb—set the current standard with 130 steals.

Not everyone can run the bases like a Henderson, Brock or Wills, but with speed once again an essential part of most teams' strategies, some ballclubs go to great lengths to achieve an edge. For spring training in 1989, the defending NL East champion New York Mets employed not only the traditional hitting, pitching and fielding instructors, but a "speed coach" as well. Steve Williams, a former world record holder in the 200 meters and the 100-yard dash, was hired to give Mets players an extra step on the bases, teaching Mookie Wilson to use his arms for greater speed and showing Lenny Dykstra how to drop the bat and shoot out of the batter's box to first base. To Mets manager Dave Johnson, hiring a speed coach was perfectly logical: "He may not make them faster, but he can make them smarter. Even half a step is an edge." ◗

Wills (opposite) proved that you don't have to be a slugger to fill the stands. In 1962 he stole a major league record 104 bases, and the Dodgers drew a major league record 2,755,184 fans. Stealing bases was back to stay.

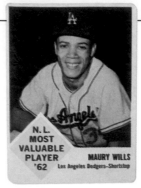

Maury Wills

After eight and a half years of bouncing around the minors from New York to Spokane, Maury Wills was an admitted baseball bum. "I was content to bounce around, not learning much, not caring much," he said. "I was sure I'd never get out of the minors." Then along came Bobby Bragan.

In July 1958 Bragan, who had been both a player and a manager in the majors, became manager of the Triple A team in Spokane, where Wills was having an ordinary season. One day during batting practice, Wills, a right-handed hitter, jumped across the plate and took two swings left-handed, missing both times. He was just fooling around, but what Bragan saw in those two swings wound up causing nightmares for everyone in the National League who didn't play for the Dodgers.

Wills was hitting around .230 when Bragan convinced him that he should become a switch-hitter. "The only thing that's kept you out of the majors is your hitting," Bragan told the 25-year-old shortstop. "If you work at it, you'll become a good switcher and that'll be your ticket to the big leagues." Wills worked at it through the summer—he hit .253 that season—then went to Venezuela to play winter ball. Wills played three or four games a week, and on his off days, he hit left-handed against anyone he could get to pitch to him. "I hit and hit and hit until my hands were sore, then put on gloves and hit some more," he said.

The work paid off. Wills got off to a hot start with Spokane in 1959, and was hitting .313 when, on June 4, he was called up to the Dodgers. Wills hit a respectable .260 in 1959, and the Dodgers won a world championship, but early in 1960 he struggled at the plate, hitting just above .200. Then along came Pete Reiser. Reiser had been a great hitter—and two-time NL base-stealing champ—with the Dodgers in the 1940s. His playing career had been cut short by his tendency to bash into concrete walls in pursuit of fly balls. Reiser became Wills' batting coach and chief motivator, working two hours with him before each game—an hour and a half on Wills' hitting and a half hour on his mental approach to the game. "Pete taught me to believe in myself," Wills said. "He gave me the inner conceit every athlete needs if he hopes to be great."

Two weeks later Wills went on a tear at the plate, and in no time, manager Walter Alston moved him from eighth to first in the batting order. Wills hit .295 that year and won his first of six straight base-stealing titles with a total of 50 stolen bases, the most in the NL since Pittsburgh's Max Carey stole 51 in 1923.

In 1962 the Dodgers moved from the L.A. Coliseum into spacious Dodger Stadium, and with runs suddenly harder to come by, Alston turned Wills loose. Now that he could get on base, Wills could concentrate on his real strengths: stealing bases and driving opponents to distraction. The Dodgers drew a major-league-record 2,755,184 fans that season, and chants of "Go, Maury, Go!" rang out all season long. As the Dodgers battled the Giants for the NL pennant, Wills battled history, chasing Ty Cobb's 1915 single-season record of 96 stolen bases. Cobb's record fell on September 23, Wills went on to steal 104 bases and the Dodgers wound up in a three-game playoff with the Giants for the pennant. Wills had four

Sliding in headfirst exposed Maury Wills to hard slap tags from opponents like Mets first baseman Ed Kranepool (7), but sometimes his legs were so battered from sliding that he had no choice. By the end of his record-breaking 1962 season, Wills said, "I was wrapped in tape like a mummy."

hits and three steals in the deciding game of the play-off, but the Giants scored four times in the ninth and went on to the World Series.

Wills' performance showed what speed could mean to a team. Despite having roughly the same team batting and slugging averages in 1962 as in 1961, the Dodgers scored 107 more runs and won 13 more games. The difference was speed; their stolen-base total went from 86 to 198—twice as many as any other team in the majors. In their pennant-winning seasons of 1963 and 1965, the Dodgers won 69.4 percent of the games in which

Wills stole at least one base. "There is no such thing as an unimportant stolen base," Wills said.

Not only had Wills brought the running game back to baseball after a 30-year absence, he put his own special slant on it. Unlike Cobb or Jackie Robinson, Wills didn't steal by intimidation. He didn't want to—and at 5′11″ and just 170 pounds, he couldn't. "I never try to bluff or rattle pitchers," Wills said. "I don't want to arouse the pitcher at all." Instead he studied pitchers and their movements, and he learned to anticipate their move to the plate in order to get the quickest start possible. "No one

Traded to the Pirates in 1967 (left), Maury Wills responded by hitting .290 with 81 steals in two years with Pittsburgh. Wills (above) was the consummate slap hitter, and 87 percent of his 2,134 career hits were singles.

gets a quicker jump on the pitcher than Wills does," said former pitcher and Giants scout Tom Sheehan, "and I pitched against Cobb." Stopping Wills was something opponents preferred not to deal with. "My instructions for preventing Wills from stealing are simple," said Reds manager Fred Hutchinson. "Don't let him get on base."

Wills' quick starts, combined with excellent raw speed, helped him succeed on 74 percent of his career attempts. In 1962, even though he was a marked man, he stole at an 88.9 percent success rate. He was a daring baserunner, but his confident, businesslike approach to base-stealing was merely an extension of his approach to his entire game. "I don't *play* baseball," he said, "I *work* baseball. This is a business, and I'm in it for the money and so are the other players."

But no other player had ever used speed to make as much money as Wills did. In 1951 he made $135 a month in the minors. By 1972—his last season in the majors—he was making $100,000 a year, a salary usually reserved for home run hitters. He used his fame to launch an off-season career as a nightclub performer, and was even getting speed-related endorsements, such as one for Delco Quick-Start batteries. He had come a long way from the slums

of Washington, D.C., where he grew up in a family of 13 children.

After a 14-year career that included four World Series and six All-Star game appearances, Wills worked as a television commentator and began managing winter league teams in Mexico. In 1977 his son, Bump, also a switch-hitter, made the majors as the Texas Rangers' starting second baseman. Late in the 1980 season Wills became baseball's third black manager, taking over the woeful Seattle Mariners. Always looking for an edge, Wills went a little too far the following April, when he had the batters' boxes at the Kingdome lengthened illegally. He was fined $500 and suspended for two games, then fired on May 6, after compiling a dismal 26–56 mark over parts of two seasons.

His lack of success as a manager wasn't too surprising. For a man who used to gauge his success by how dirty his uniform got, sitting in the dugout and watching just didn't make it. "If my uniform isn't dirty," he once said, "I haven't done my job." His job was stealing bases, and he did it so well that he changed the face of the game. Of his record-breaking 104 steals in 1962, Wills said, "I'll tell you how much it changed baseball. In 1965 I stole 94 bases and no one said hardly a word about it."

Intensity turned Wills from a complacent minor leaguer into a major league star. "In the off-season he's relaxed, but during the season he's a different guy," said Bruce Innes, a songwriter who worked with Wills on a nightclub act. "Sometimes he's almost incoherent."

MAURY WILLS

Shortstop
Los Angeles Dodgers 1959–1966, 1969–1972
Pittsburgh Pirates 1967–1968
Montreal Expos 1969

GAMES	**1,942**
AT-BATS	**7,588**
BATTING AVERAGE	
Career	**.281**
Season High	**.302**
SLUGGING AVERAGE	
Career	**.331**
Season High	**.373**
HITS	
Career	**2,134**
Season High	**208**
DOUBLES	
Career	**177**
Season High	**19**
TRIPLES	
Career	**71**
Season High	**10**
HOME RUNS	
Career	**20**
Season High	**6**
RUNS BATTED IN	
Career	**458**
Season High	**48**
RUNS	
Career	**1,067**
Season High	**130**
STOLEN BASES	
Career	**586**
Season High *(7th all time)*	**104**
STOLEN-BASE TITLES, NL	**1960–1965**
WORLD SERIES	**1959, 1963, 1965, 1966**
MOST VALUABLE PLAYER	**1962**

Wills' speed led the NL to a 3–1 win over the AL in the 1962 All-Star Game. In the sixth Wills stole second and scored on a single, then in the eighth he singled, went to third on a single to left and scored (above) on a short foul fly to right.

Speedsters

The only constant in baseball is speed.

—Maury Wills

There is no hurry-up offense, no two-minute drill, no shot clock —indeed, there is no clock at all to rush the game along. Still, baseball, as much as any other team sport, rewards speed. So baseball scouts arm themselves with radar guns and stopwatches when hunting down the best prospects. With a pitcher, the question is, how fast can he throw; with an infielder, how quick are his reflexes; with an outfielder, how much ground can he cover? And when it comes to offense, can he make it to first in 4.3 seconds or less?

A quality pitching prospect should be able to throw a fastball at the major league average—about 85 miles an hour. To be sure, there are a handful of contemporary pitchers who have survived, and even flourished, without this kind of speed—knuckleballers and finesse pitchers like Frank Tanana, who, after impressing California Angels scouts with his speed, was forced to change his pitching style after an arm injury. The scouts will tell you that speed alone is rarely enough to make it in the big leagues. But they will also tell you that in today's game, those who throw the hardest—fireballing starters like Nolan Ryan or Roger Clemens and flamethrowing stoppers like Jeff Reardon or Mitch Williams—set the standard.

It wasn't always so. In the earliest days of baseball, the rules didn't even factor speed into the pitching equation. "The ball must be pitched, not thrown, for the bat," wrote Alexander Cartwright, who compiled the first rule book for baseball in 1845. As a result, early pitchers used a stiff-armed,

The base-stealer of the 1990s runs with power, and the prototype is Kansas City's Bo Jackson (opposite). At 6' 1" and 222 pounds, Jackson is a world-class sprinter, and he combined his power and speed for 32 home runs and 26 stolen bases in 1989.

Dwight Gooden's 95 mph fastball starts with a powerful leg drive and often ends in the catcher's mitt. The Mets' ace right-hander set a major league rookie record with 276 strikeouts in 1984.

underhand motion, virtually lobbing the ball to the plate. It wasn't too long, however, before pitchers realized that they might gain an edge if they could figure out some way to bend the rules in order to get some speed on the ball. And since the mound was some 15 feet closer to home plate than it is now, it didn't require a great deal of power to overwhelm the batter.

A series of rule changes in the 1870s increased the importance of pitching speed. In 1872 the wrist snap was legalized. The requirement that the pitcher's arm swing perpendicular to the ground was also eased, spawning a generation of hurlers who threw from below the hip, Dan Quisenberry-style. By 1875 Tommy Bond of Hartford raised his sidearm delivery above the waist, intimidating batters with his fastball. Soon, pitchers were generating even greater speed with a three-quarter, from-the-shoulder motion. Despite warnings from league officials and a few forfeits, the practice continued, and by 1894 all restrictions preventing a full overhand delivery were removed.

One of the beneficiaries of this series of rule changes was Amos Rusie. Rusie, known as "the Hoosier Thunderbolt," revolutionized the game in the 1890s as Babe Ruth did in the 1920s. His fastballs and curves were thrown so hard that batters feared for their lives, and rulemakers feared that if they didn't increase the distance between pitcher and batter, someone might be killed. So in 1893 the distance from the pitcher's mound to home plate expanded from 50 feet to the current distance of 60 feet 6 inches.

During the dead-ball era, from 1901 to 1919, pitchers who didn't have Rusie's speed might survive by scuffing the ball or throwing a spitter, but the fastball was still coveted. Walter Johnson was the new century's first strikeout king. How fast was he? Legend has it that on a dark afternoon, catcher Eddie Ainsmith walked to the mound and told Johnson to fake the

Nolan Ryan's fastball was once timed at 100.9 mph, but all most hitters know is that they can't hit it. In 1989, at the age of 42, Ryan (left) allowed an average of just 6.1 hits per nine innings. Fifty-eight years earlier, Lefty Grove (below) rode baseball's best fastball to a 31–4 mark, allowing 7.8 hits per nine innings.

pitch. Johnson wound up, but did not throw the ball. Ainsmith thumped his catcher's glove, and the umpire called strike three.

Negro league star Satchel Paige was never timed with a radar gun, but if legend is any measure of speed, he probably threw just as fast as Johnson had. After one batter was called out on a Paige fastball, he turned around and said, "That one sounded a little low, didn't it, ump?"

In recent years, pitching has become more and more specialized, placing an even greater premium on speed. A starting pitcher who is backed up by a strong reliever can throw harder than if he had to pace himself to go the full nine innings. And when a reliever with a 95 mph fastball knows he is going to face only a few batters, he does not have to worry so much about burning out his arm by throwing heat.

With position players there are more variables. Scouts assess skills in the field, at the plate and on the bases. Different teams have different criteria, but Toronto Blue Jays scout Chris Bourjos says that "number one is speed."

Just as some pitchers have succeeded without tremendous fastballs, some infielders and outfielders have succeeded with average or below-average foot speed. But the player or team with great defensive speed has a distinct advantage, particularly in today's age of spacious, artificial-turf ballparks. Indeed, a fast defensive team can help a not-so-fast pitcher thrive. Struggling for six years with Boston and Pittsburgh, clubs with mediocre defense, John Tudor compiled a less-than-earthshaking record of 51 wins and 43 losses. Traded to the Cardinals before the 1985 season, he suddenly blossomed, compiling a 21–8 record, with ten shutouts and a 1.93 ERA.

5′ 9″ 170 lbs.
BR TR

b 10/18/1881
d 9/14/1968

HANS LOBERT
Third Base

When he was 15, Hans Lobert used his Christmas money, $3.50, to buy his first pair of baseball spikes. Unable to wait for spring, he put them on as soon as he got home and danced outside in the falling snow. Lobert went on to steal 316 bases in his major league career, but fans remember him for his childlike enthusiasm, his humor and his race against a horse.

Lobert broke into the majors with Pittsburgh in 1903 and was a solid third baseman for several NL teams during his 14-year career. He had a lifetime .274 average, but his greatest asset was his speed; he stole 30 or more bases seven times. Although he never played for a World Series winner, his skills were recognized by some of the game's great figures, like Giant manager John McGraw. McGraw put Lobert on his barnstorming team for a 1913 world tour. On the American leg of the tour, in Oxnard, California, Lobert starred in a bizarre contest.

It had been announced to the fans that Lobert—who held the record of 13.8 seconds for circling the diamond—would race a horse around the bases. The local fans placed their bets, and in front of a rowdy crowd, Lobert and the horse took off. Lobert got an early lead, but the horse crowded him between second and third. Lobert was unable to recover, and the horse just edged him out. Umpire Bill Klem announced that the horse had won by a nose. But Lobert, referring to his own rather prominent nose, said "that was highly unlikely."

Honus Wagner's nickname—"the Flying Dutchman"—was well earned. The Pirate star led the NL five times in stolen bases, tied a World Series record with six steals in 1909, and in 1915, at the age of 41, still managed to steal 22 bases.

What accounted for the turnaround? Tudor claims that he was the same pitcher he had always been, but that playing in ample Busch Stadium with the speedy St. Louis defense made him more confident on the mound. "I'm not going to overpower anybody," he adds. "I'm the kind of pitcher who has to keep the ball in play, and knowing the Cardinals' defense was behind me really helped." Confident in those behind him, a pitcher doesn't have to be as fine with his pitches. That means fewer walks, which usually means fewer runs.

Fast reflexes are essential to star at third base, the hot corner, but scouts look for both quickness and speed afoot in those who play up the middle—in center field, at shortstop and at second base. Tudor was blessed with Gold Glove center fielder Willie McGee and shortstop nonpareil Ozzie Smith. Chasing down almost anything hit his way, McGee carried on baseball's long tradition of speedy center fielders dating back to Bill Lange in the 19th century, Tris Speaker, Oscar Charleston and Max Carey in the early years of the 20th century, and more recent defensive greats like Willie Mays and Paul Blair. Smith's remarkable range calls to mind earlier shortstops like Hall of Famers Rabbit Maranville, Honus Wagner and "Little Looie" Aparicio.

It is easy to measure a pitcher's speed with a radar gun, but how do scouts gauge the quickness of a position player? One way is by timing how long it takes a player to run from home to first. A right-handed batter should be able to make it in 4.3 seconds, a left-hander in .1 second less. One-tenth of a second may not seem like much, but over the years, a large number of right-handers have learned to switch-hit to take advantage of the left-hander's shorter trip to first base.

Shortstop Ozzie Smith makes highlight reels with his acrobatic fielding, but his speed on the basepaths helps keep the Cardinal machine in high gear. Smith stole 432 bases in his first 12 years in the majors and had a success rate of 80.4 percent.

Stealing home was a specialty of Brooklyn outfielder Pete Reiser. Reiser slid under Cubs catcher Salvador Hernandez (above) to give the Dodgers the lead in a 1942 game, then four years later set a major league record by stealing home seven times in a season.

But whether a player bats right or left, making it to first in anything under four seconds excites a scout. The reason is simple: having a speedster in the lineup creates runs when the team is at bat and prevents them when the team is in the field. The World Series alone provides a host of examples. In the 1946 Series, the Cardinals' Enos Slaughter scored all the way from first base on a Harry Walker hit to beat the Red Sox, four games to three. In the opening game of the 1954 Series, the Giants' Willie Mays raced to the center field wall and made a spectacular catch, robbing the Indians' Vic Wertz of a hit with two men on. Aggressive baserunning by Pepper Martin in 1931 and Lou Brock in 1967 led the Cardinals to Series victories.

Speed has been celebrated since baseball's beginnings. In the game's first half century—from the days of Harry Wright's Cincinnati Red Stockings to the end of World War I—speed was the critical element of the game. As late as 1918, Francis Richter's *Reach Guide* noted that, "on the ball field speed counts for more than actual physical power in the way of brute strength."

That speed was more important than power in those early years was a reflection of the times. Baseball grew into its own during an age in which science also became increasingly important and popular, and scientific principles were applied to almost anything. In the 1870s teams were drilled until they functioned like the efficient machines of the Industrial Revolution. Henry Chadwick, considered by many to be the "Father of Baseball," argued for a game in which runs would be scored by place-hitting, bunting and stealing bases; pitching and defense would protect the lead. Brains rather than brawn were to be rewarded.

But Chadwick was not without critics. The proponents of what was called "the manly game" invoked the survival-of-the-fittest concept to call for more slugging and more aggressive play. They argued that fans would rather watch a display of strength and power than the "effeminate" game espoused by Chadwick.

The battle between the two schools came to a head in the winter of 1892, when major league baseball's rules committee debated the distance between home plate and the pitching rubber. Philadelphia Phillies manager Harry Wright and his followers argued that the distance of the day, 50 feet, be kept to ensure that scientific baseball would continue to flourish. Opponents wanted to make the distance 63 feet, a sure bet to increase manly slugging. In the end, a compromise—the present 60 feet 6 inches—became the standard.

Cincinnati's Pete Rose was no speed merchant, but his aggressiveness and hustle made him a dangerous baserunner. His career high in steals was 20, but he scored at least 100 runs ten times.

Many of the strategies advocated by the scientific school play an important role in the game to this day. The bunt, for example, is the offspring of the fair-foul hit, invented by Dickey Pearce. Pearce purposely hit the ball so that it bounced first in fair territory and then went foul; at the time, such a hit was ruled fair, even if it went foul before reaching first or third base. The origin of the stolen base is unknown, but it was also an integral part of the scientific game, especially toward the end of the 19th century. In 1888 Harry Stovey of the Philadelphia Athletics of the old American Association stole 87 bases, and in 1891 Sliding Billy Hamilton set a National League record stealing 156 bases playing for the Philadelphia Phillies. But a stolen base then was not what it is today.

In 1886, the first year official records were kept, runners were credited with a steal every time they reached the next base without the aid of a hit, a

Continued on page 30

Billy Hamilton

His two nicknames tell it all: "Good Eye Billy" and "Sliding Billy." During his 14 seasons in the majors—from 1888 through 1901—Billy Hamilton was the most efficient leadoff hitter in baseball.

Leadoff hitters not only have to get on base, they have to get into position to score. Hamilton excelled at both tasks. He earned the nickname Good Eye Billy because he seldom struck out and rarely swung at bad pitches; he also led the National League in walks five times.

If a pitcher put the ball over the plate and Hamilton wasn't happy with it, he simply hit it foul; he once fouled off 29 consecutive pitches while waiting for one he liked. This strategy paid off in more than walks; he was consistently among the NL's top hitters, compiling a .344 lifetime average. Of his 2,163 hits, four out of five were singles.

Once on base, Good Eye Billy became Sliding Billy, who tormented opponents with his speed and daring. Playing for Philadelphia in 1894, he stole seven bases in a single game against Washington. On another afternoon, Cleveland's third baseman became so incensed watching Sliding Billy advance at will from base to base that he picked up the short, stocky Hamilton, carried him to the edge of the field and dumped him into the grandstand.

Hamilton led the NL in stolen bases six times. His single-season record of 117, set in 1889 when he was with Kansas City in the American Association, survived until Lou Brock stole 118 in 1974. And Hamilton's career total of 937 steals was the record for nearly a century, until Lou Brock amassed 938 over 19 seasons.

Of course, the rules were slightly different in Hamilton's days. A heads-up baserunner who took an "extra" base—going from first to third on the batter's single or first to home on a double—was credited with a steal. So perhaps a more convincing measurement of Hamilton's proficiency was his ability to score runs. During his career, Hamilton played in 1,593 games and scored 1,692 runs—which means that he scored an average of more than one run per game. The last time a major leaguer was able to score more than one run per game *in a single season* was 1936, when Lou Gehrig crossed the plate 167 times in 155 games. Yet Billy Hamilton did it nine times in 14 years.

In addition to his offensive skills, Hamilton was an outstanding center fielder who was known for his quick starts and acrobatic off-balance catches.

After his first two seasons with the Kansas City Blues, the franchise folded and Hamilton went to the Philadelphia Phillies. Four years later he set a record for runs scored in a single season—196—that has never been broken. The next year he hit .389 and led the league in runs, walks and stolen bases. Yet when he asked for a modest salary increase, he was traded to Boston, where he helped the Beaneaters win pennants in 1897 and 1898.

When Hamilton retired from the majors he became a manager for the New England League—and he made baseball a family affair. He and his wife had four daughters, and when one of them was in the third grade, her teacher asked her, "Ethel, do you know what happened in the world in 1898?" "Why, yes," she answered. "That was the year Dewey took Manila and Boston took the pennant."

OLD JUDGE CIGARETTES Goodwin & Co., New York.

At 5' 6" and 165 pounds, Billy Hamilton was among the game's stockiest—and best—base-stealers. Hamilton, who ran a 10.75 in the 100-yard dash in high school, set a team record with 93 steals in 1896, his first season with the Boston Beaneaters.

BILLY
HAMILTON

Outfield
Kansas City Blues 1888–1889
Philadelphia Phillies 1890–1895
Boston Beaneaters 1896–1901
Hall of Fame 1961

GAMES	1,593
AT-BATS	6,284

BATTING AVERAGE	
Career *(9th all time)*	.344
Season High	.399

SLUGGING AVERAGE	
Career	.432
Season High	.524

HITS	
Career	2,163
Season High	223

DOUBLES	
Career	242
Season High	25

TRIPLES	
Career	94
Season High	15

HOME RUNS	
Career	40
Season High	7

RUNS BATTED IN	
Career	736
Season High	87

RUNS	
Career	1,692
Season High *(1st all time)*	196

STOLEN BASES	
Career	937*
Season High	117*

STOLEN-BASE TITLES,	
AA	1889
NL	1890, 1891, 1894–1896, 1898

* Includes stolen bases credited under pre-1899 rules.

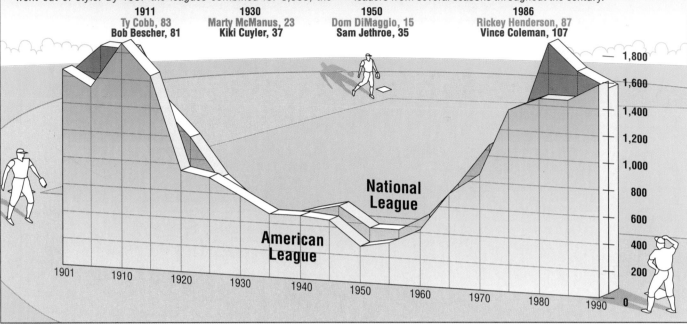

The Fall and Rise of Running

Stolen bases meant something at the beginning of the 20th century, but from the 1920s until the early 1960s, stealing bases went out of style. By 1987 the leagues combined for 3,585, the most in the century, but not many more than the 3,404 swiped in 1911. Below is a chart of the leagues' stolen base totals, with league leaders from several seasons throughout the century.

1911
Ty Cobb, 83
Bob Bescher, 81

1930
Marty McManus, 23
Kiki Cuyler, 37

1950
Dom DiMaggio, 15
Sam Jethroe, 35

1986
Rickey Henderson, 87
Vince Coleman, 107

National League

American League

1901 1910 1920 1930 1940 1950 1960 1970 1980 1990

1,800
1,600
1,400
1,200
1,000
800
600
400
200
0

Outfielder Hugh Duffy is best known for his .438 batting average with Boston in 1894, the highest single-season mark of all time. But he was also a fine base-stealer and averaged 56 steals a season from 1889 to 1897.

walk, a balk, a wild pitch or a passed ball. If anyone made a throwing error trying to catch the runner, or if the fielder dropped the ball in making a tag, a steal was credited. If a runner overran or overslid the base and was then tagged out, he was still credited with a steal. Stealing itself was also easier because catchers, lacking today's equipment and fearing injury, played farther behind the plate than they now do. It was not until 1907, for example, that New York Giants catcher Roger Bresnahan introduced shin guards.

In 1892 the stolen-base rule was expanded so that, "If a baserunner advances a base on a fly out, or gains two bases on a single hit, or an infield out or an attempted out, he shall be credited with a stolen base, provided there is a possible chance and a palpable attempt to retire him." In an age of low-scoring games, rulemakers clearly gave importance to gaining an extra base. A player who could advance his team's cause by moving from first to third on a single was rewarded in the box score. It wasn't until 1898 that the stolen base was defined as it is today, and since then there have been only minor changes. Only when a runner reaches the base he attempts to steal unaided by a fielding or battery error, or a hit by the batter, is he credited with a stolen base.

The most celebrated base-stealer at the turn of the century—perhaps the first player to become a hero because of his aggressiveness on the bases —was Billy Hamilton, who played center field with Kansas City, Philadelphia and Boston from 1888 to 1901. His statistics are impressive, despite the then liberal rules for determining stolen bases. He led the National League in steals six times and the American Association once, and recorded 937 career steals.

But Hamilton was by no means a one-dimensional player: he was nearly as good a hitter as he was a baserunner. He batted a career .344, won two

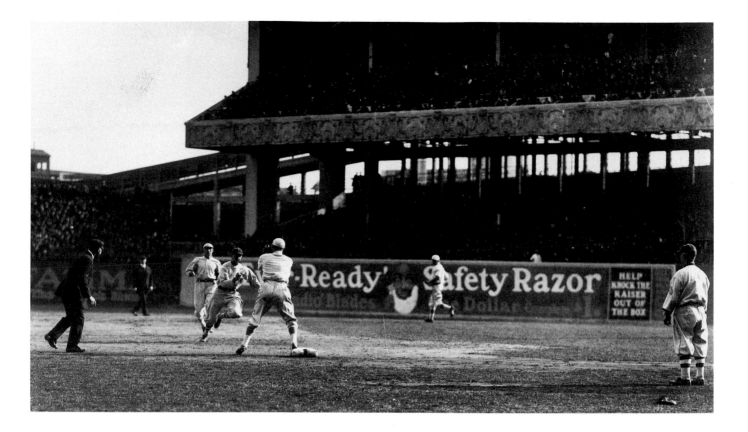

batting titles and once compiled a 36-game hitting streak—the fifth highest total in NL history. The combination of skills proved costly for opposing teams: in 1894, while batting .399, Hamilton scored 196 runs—a record that still stands. Those numbers are, at least in part, a result of having good hitters behind him. But there is no doubt that Hamilton's own skills were outstanding.

For all his success, however, Hamilton apparently never got over the fact that Ty Cobb was generally considered the greatest base-stealer in history, credited with the most steals in a season—96—and the most career steals—892. In December of 1937, at the age of 71, Hamilton wrote a letter of protest to the editor of *The Sporting News:*

Dear Sir:

In the November 16th issue of your paper you made reference to Billy Hamilton of the old Philadelphia and Boston NL clubs of the 1890s as one of the prolific base stealers of the 19th century. I'll have you know sir that I was and will be the greatest stealer of all times. I did stole over 100 bases on many years and if they ever re-count the record I will get my just reward.

Very Truly
Sliding Billy Hamilton

The record has never been re-counted, but Hamilton was elected to the Hall of Fame posthumously in 1961.

Second baseman Eddie Collins was called "the smartest player who ever lived" by former Athletics teammate Rube Bressler, but even the best sometimes get caught. Collins, who also played for the White Sox and stole 743 bases in his career, got picked off second in Game 4 of the 1917 World Series (above) and was tagged out by Giants third baseman Heinie Zimmerman. Still, Collins' White Sox won the Series in six.

A rundown is one of baseball's most patterned and chaotic plays. The runner, in this case Milwaukee's Paul Molitor, tries to prolong the rundown to increase his chance of escaping and to allow other runners to advance. The team in the field, having practiced rundowns during spring training, now tries to remember who's supposed to back up whom. Here, Cleveland pitcher Dan Spillner (37) and third baseman Toby Harrah do the chasing.

Hamilton's lifetime on-base percentage of .455 is fourth on the all-time list, just behind John McGraw's .460. McGraw played the infield for the Baltimore Orioles as aggressively as he managed the New York Giants. The Orioles of the 1890s used speed and strategy—and a little skulduggery—to win games in the dead-ball era, when runs were few and far between. McGraw and his teammates are traditionally given credit for such innovations as the Baltimore chop and the hit-and-run—two of the best-known tactics for manufacturing runs. The Baltimore chop was perfected by Wee Willie Keeler when he played for Baltimore in the mid-1890s. Standing stiff-legged, leaning over the plate, the diminutive Keeler chopped down on the ball, making it bounce so high that before it came down, he had easily reached first base. As for the hit-and-run, baseball's revisionist historian Bill James suggests that although McGraw and his cohorts used it, the Boston Beaneaters actually invented the ploy. John Montgomery Ward, a multiposition player who also managed the Giants, described how it was done in Boston: "The man on first makes a bluff attempt to steal second, but runs back to first. By this it becomes known whether the second baseman or the short stop is going to cover second for the throw from the catcher. Then the batsman gets the signal from the man on first that [he] is going to steal on a certain pitched ball. The moment he starts for second the batsman just pushes the ball for the place occupied only a moment before by the infielder who has gone to cover second base." This is, of course, the hit-and-run as we now know it.

Ironically, an even more imaginative application of scientific principles was demonstrated by one of the zaniest ballplayers of any era, Herman "Germany" Schaefer. Schaefer played with the Detroit Tigers—usually at second base—during some of their greatest years, from 1905 to 1908.

With superstars Ty Cobb and Sam Crawford battling for the spotlight in the outfield, the Tigers kept Schaefer around, mostly because he provided comic relief. But in the late innings of a tie game versus the Cleveland Indians on September 4, 1908, he made his mark in baseball history by stealing first base, and won the game in the process. With Schaefer on first base, speedster Davy Jones on third and Sam Crawford at the plate, Schaefer flashed Jones the sign for a double steal, hoping to draw a throw to second base to clear the way for Jones to score. But Cleveland catcher Nig Clarke wisely held the ball and allowed Schaefer to take second uncontested. On the next pitch, Schaefer, not yet ready to admit defeat, let out a scream and headed back to first. More than 50 years later, Jones described the incident to interviewer Lawrence Ritter: "Everybody just stood there . . . with their mouths open, not knowing what the devil was going on. Me, too. Even if the catcher *had* thrown to first, I was too stunned to move, I'll tell you that."

Perhaps Schaefer believed that the third time is the charm, because on the next pitch he screamed again, put his head down and set out to regain second base. Clarke felt that he had taken enough abuse for one day; he *did* throw to second that time, but too late to get Schaefer, and in the meantime Jones was able to score the go-ahead run. It was not until 1920 that the rules were amended to prohibit running the bases "in reverse order for the purpose either of confusing the fielders or making a travesty of the game."

Cobb broke into the major leagues in 1905, and he played with such style that the period is often called the Cobb era—a time when speed was clearly more important than power. But by the 1920s, baseball was in the Ruth

Rookie of the Year in 1985, White Sox shortstop Ozzie Guillen has been dazzling in the field: in 1988 Guillen broke the team record for assists by a shortstop—held by Hall of Famer Luis Aparicio. But he compares less favorably with Aparicio on the basepaths: although he stole 25 bases in 1988, he was caught 13 times.

Even though he makes about $4 million a year, the Giants' Will Clark isn't afraid to sacrifice his body—or St. Louis' Tommy Herr's—to break up a double play.

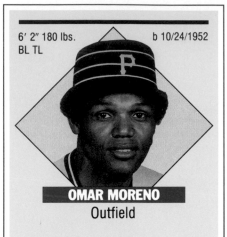

6′ 2″ 180 lbs. b 10/24/1952
BL TL

OMAR MORENO
Outfield

Omar Moreno was known for his aggressive baserunning. But Pittsburgh manager Chuck Tanner gave Moreno credit for "being able to do so many things. He gives us outstanding defense. He plays every day. He has improved as a hitter and he can only get better."

In 1977, his first full season with the Pirates, Moreno displayed his speed on the basepaths, stealing 53 bases in 69 attempts. But he hit only .240. The next year he led the NL in stolen bases with 71 and hit just .235. The Pirates, wanting to use Moreno in the leadoff spot, called in former Pirate manager and NL batting champ Harry Walker.

Walker spent three weeks working with Moreno, and he got results. In 1979 Moreno had 196 hits, 110 runs scored, 69 RBI, a career-high .282 average *and* a league-leading 77 stolen bases. His performance in the leadoff spot fired up the team, and the Pirates, three-time second-place finishers since 1975, became the 1979 world champions. Catcher Steve Nicosia explained, "the key to our club is Omar."

In 1980 Moreno stole a career-high 96 bases and went on to steal a total of 487 bases over his 12-year career. He ranks 16th on the all-time list.

Although Moreno was aggressive on the basepaths, he was soft-spoken and modest off the field. Teammate Phil Garner, an infielder, said, "He's a quiet man who simply gets the job done."

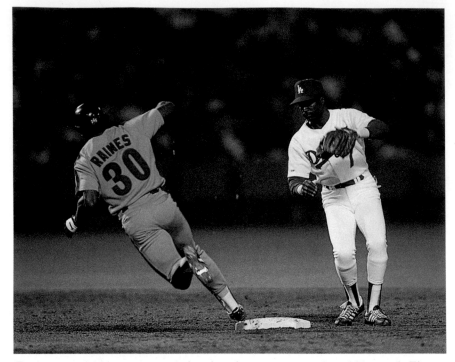

For a successful baserunner, technique is as important as speed, and Montreal's Tim Raines possesses both. Here, Raines rounds second with his outside foot to cut yards off a trip around the bases. Raines made that trip a league-leading 133 times in 1983.

era. In 1921 the change was already apparent to sportswriter F. C. Lane, who wrote in *Baseball Magazine* of "basestealing's sensational decline." Lane cited statistics showing an "ominous" fall in the number of steals, and he noted that in 1921 the Tigers stole a meager 95 bases, one less than Cobb alone had stolen in 1915. "The last few seasons have seen a falling off in basestealing so pronounced as to prove alarming to anyone who wishes to see baseball preserved as a game well rounded in every department," wrote Lane.

Thirty-five years later, Lane would have been able to find even more statistical grist for his mill. The game in which speed was paramount was carried on in the Negro leagues in the 1920s, 1930s and 1940s, but with very few exceptions—notably, the St. Louis Cardinals and the Brooklyn Dodgers —manly slugging had completely overwhelmed scientific baseball in the major leagues.

The arrival of Jackie Robinson and other black players in the major leagues in the late 1940s heralded a return to the well-rounded game, but it really wasn't until Luis Aparicio came to the Chicago White Sox in 1956 that the art of base-stealing was finally revived. Hailing from Venezuela, where baseball had been introduced by barnstorming black professionals in the dead-ball era, Aparicio was propelled to stardom by his speed. A smooth fielder, he led American League shortstops in fielding eight years and won nine Gold Gloves. His speed gave him great range, and that guaranteed that he was always among the league leaders in chances, putouts and assists. His numbers on the bases were just as impressive. He led the American League in steals in each of his first nine seasons, and in 1959 his

total of 56—in just 69 attempts—was the most since George Case had stolen 61 in 1943. In fact, it was the fifth best total in the league since Cobb stole his record 96. As a result of their aggressive dead-ball style of play, the "Go-Go" Sox of Aparicio, Nellie Fox and Jim Landis toppled the Yankees from their perennial position in first place.

After Aparicio there was the unforgettable Maury Wills and after Wills there was Lou Brock and after Brock there is Rickey Henderson. Henderson not only broke both Brock's single-season and career stolen base records, he did both at younger ages than Brock. In 1982, at the tender age of 24, Henderson smashed Brock's single-season record of 118—set at age 35—with 130 steals. Wills was 29 when he broke Cobb's single-season record in 1962, a record Cobb had set in 1915 at age 28. And on May 1, 1991, Henderson stole his 939th base, establishing a new career total that reached 994 by season's end.

Baseball savants consider Henderson more daring and aggressive than either Brock or Wills. That daring, he says, is a product of his childhood: "I used to be a crazy kind of kid, and I guess this daredevil stuff is just a carryover. I'd climb up a tree and then fall out and then I'd try to climb the tree again. When I played ball as a kid in Oakland all I cared about was getting to the next base. I learned never to be afraid of being thrown out." Of course he *has* been thrown out. In 1982 he was caught stealing a record 42 times, but his success ratio was still over 75 percent that year, and his lifetime success rate is over 80 percent. And there's nothing wrong with Henderson's power at the plate. He has hit as many as 28 home runs in a season and trails only Bobby Bonds in the number of lifetime leadoff home runs.

Few players were concerned with stealing bases in the homer-happy 1940s, but Washington's George Case (above, stealing home against Athletics catcher Bob Swift with Washington's Bob Johnson looking on) was one of them. Case led the AL in steals six times from 1939 to 1946.

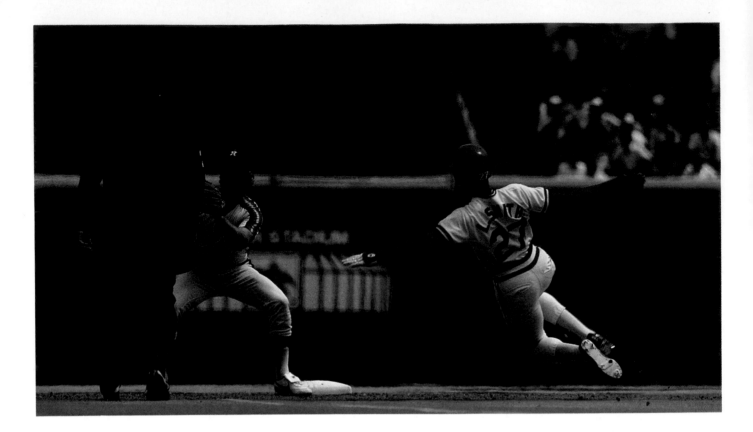

Lonnie Smith's speed paid off quickly for two Missouri teams. In 1982, Smith's first year with St. Louis (above), he stole 68 bases and led the NL with 120 runs scored, and the Cardinals won a world championship. Early in 1985 he was traded to Kansas City, where he stole 40 bases and helped the Royals win another world championship.

Billy Martin—who managed Henderson in Oakland and as Yankees manager persuaded club owner George Steinbrenner to trade for Henderson—named Henderson to his personal all-time squad along with Mickey Mantle and Willie Mays in the outfield. Martin made no apologies for choosing Henderson ahead of such greats as Al Kaline, Carl Yastrzemski, Frank Robinson, Stan Musial, Hank Aaron and Roberto Clemente: "Rickey is a once-in-a-lifetime player. You see very few Rickey Hendersons. You might not see another one for fifty years. He has to be the greatest leadoff man in the history of baseball. There has never been a leadoff man like him with his power and speed."

Power and speed: that combination—a fusion of the skills inherited from both the lively-ball and the dead-ball eras—has made baseball today the well-rounded game that F. C. Lane longed for back in 1921. ◖

Second baseman Willie Randolph (opposite) came out of the gate flying with the Yankees in 1976, and stole 37 bases that season, his career high. In 1980 Randolph had a .429 on-base percentage for the Yankees, led the AL with 119 walks and stole 30 bases.

Bobby Bonds

Instant success in the major leagues is every rookie's dream, but, as Bobby Bonds found out, it can also be a burden. He came to the San Francisco Giants in June 1968 and hit a grand slam in his first game. It was an extraordinary beginning, and the baseball world began to watch him with extraordinary expectations.

If Bonds fell a little short of those expectations, it was not because he failed to mature as a player in the majors but because he was mature when he arrived. In his first full season with the Giants, he performed at a level he maintained through most of his 14-year career—an average of about 30 home runs and 40 stolen bases a season. In fact, he stole 45 bases in his rookie season and was thrown out only four times, a feat that belied his lack of experience. The next five years turned out to be the finest of his career. In 1973 he fell just one long ball shy of being the first major leaguer to hit 40 homers and steal 40 bases in the same season. In 1971, under the guidance of Willie Mays, he took home the first of three Gold Gloves for his play in right field.

Perhaps the only drawback to his play in those years was his tendency to strike out. In 1969 he set a record by fanning 187 times. The next season that record fell to number two on the all-time list when Bonds whiffed 189 times. "I'm not the type of hitter to choke up and just tap the ball with two strikes on me," declared the unrepentant strikeout king. In 1974 Reds manager Sparky Anderson endorsed Bonds' hit-or-miss style, declaring him "the best ballplayer in America."

Many owners, managers and coaches thought Bonds would blossom from a superstar into a virtual superman. This made him more valuable on the trading block than on the field, and he played the final seven years of his career with seven different teams. Another reason for Bonds' team-hopping was the birth of the free-agency era. Owners like Bill Veeck of Chicago, where Bonds played for part of 1978, figured that Bonds would ask for more money than the team could afford and decided to trade him for younger, cheaper talent.

The frequent trades made it difficult for Bonds to establish an identity with the fans in one region or league. This lack of identity made him less of a drawing card than he deserved to be and increased the likelihood of more trades. But Bonds was as much responsible for his dilemma as anyone else. Although he never lacked the drive to excel, he just didn't know how to blow his own horn. "Shoot," he shrugged, "people wouldn't believe the Messiah when he said he was God. They sure aren't going to believe me." Testimony to Bonds' under appreciated skills was his failure to make the 1977 All-Star team even though he led the AL in homers and was second in both RBI and stolen bases as the midseason break approached.

When Bonds retired in 1981, he left one record that may stand for a long time: he hit at least 30 home runs and stole at least 30 bases in the same season five times: in 1969, 1973, 1975, 1977 and 1978. Only Howard Johnson had accomplished the feat three times—Willie Mays and Ron Gant did it twice. Bonds may not be a household name among the next generation of baseball fans, but he sees a kind of charm in that—even if it's the charm of a consolation prize. "Someday," he said proudly, "people are going to look in the record book and say, 'Who in the hell was Bobby Bonds?'"

Bobby Bonds was traded or sold seven times in his career, but the moves didn't dampen his aggressiveness on the bases or his self-confidence. "If they can trade Willie Mays and Babe Ruth, they can trade anybody," he said.

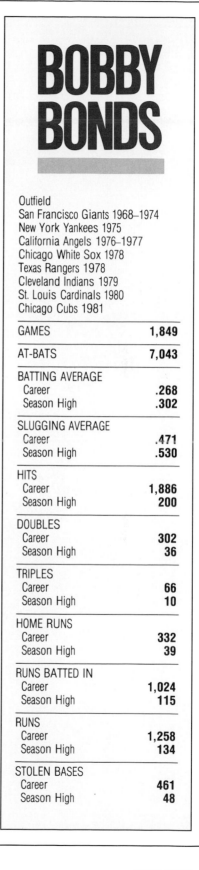

BOBBY BONDS

Outfield
San Francisco Giants 1968–1974
New York Yankees 1975
California Angels 1976–1977
Chicago White Sox 1978
Texas Rangers 1978
Cleveland Indians 1979
St. Louis Cardinals 1980
Chicago Cubs 1981

GAMES	1,849
AT-BATS	7,043
BATTING AVERAGE	
Career	.268
Season High	.302
SLUGGING AVERAGE	
Career	.471
Season High	.530
HITS	
Career	1,886
Season High	200
DOUBLES	
Career	302
Season High	36
TRIPLES	
Career	66
Season High	10
HOME RUNS	
Career	332
Season High	39
RUNS BATTED IN	
Career	1,024
Season High	115
RUNS	
Career	1,258
Season High	134
STOLEN BASES	
Career	461
Season High	48

The Georgia
Peach

Ty Cobb (below) grew up under the dominating influence of a father whose career included stints as school principal, mayor, newspaper publisher and state senator. When young Ty chose baseball as a profession—over his father's objections—the elder Cobb told him, "Don't come home a failure." He didn't, and in 1914 (right) he won his eighth straight batting title.

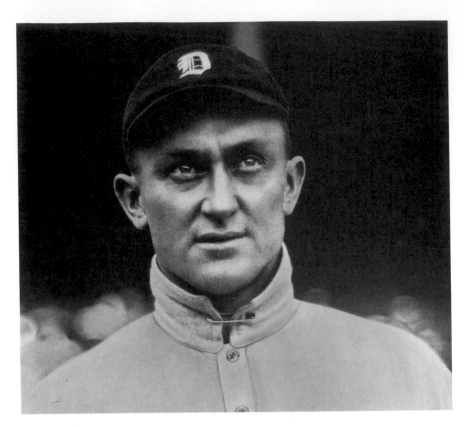

When Detroit's Ty Cobb spiked Philadelphia's Home Run Baker in the midst of the tight 1909 pennant race (preceding page), the event touched off a hail of criticism. The photo seems to support Cobb's claim that the spiking was unintentional—Baker was far from agile—but the next time the Tigers visited Philadelphia, Cobb received death threats and had to be escorted to and from the ballpark by police.

oward the end of a ballgame between the Philadelphia Athletics and the Detroit Tigers, manager Connie Mack turned to veteran catcher Ira Thomas and said, "Keep a tight hold on that glove of yours, or Cobb will be stealing it before you get out of the park." He was only half joking; Cobb had stolen everything else. Cobb led off the first inning of the July 12, 1911, game by getting a walk off A's pitcher Harry Krause. As the next batter struck out, Cobb stole second. But that was nothing unusual; the A's had been expecting him to steal. When the third batter struck out and Cobb stole third, Krause finally relaxed, thinking that Cobb had done all the damage he was going to do—he wouldn't dare steal home. "The Georgia Peach" was standing close to third base, looking as though he, too, was content with two steals. But as soon as Krause committed himself toward home, Cobb was off, and wound up beating a high pitch to the plate. Describing the game, E. A. Batchelor of the *Detroit Free Press* echoed Connie Mack's sentiments that Cobb was unstoppable: "Whoever wrote the rules carelessly prohibited the stealing of first base, so Ty couldn't grab that one."

Whether he was flying into a base with his spikes high or executing perfect bunts or slapping the ball past pulled-in infielders or lining it beyond outfielders and then taking the extra base, Cobb was an unforgettable figure to those who saw him play. There was no love lost between Cobb and the Athletics, yet Rube Bressler, who pitched for the Athletics while Cobb was in Detroit said, "Cobb had that terrific fire, that unbelievable drive. His determination was fantastic. I never saw anybody like him. It was his base. It was his game. Everything was his." The fire that Bressler saw burned throughout Cobb's 24 years in the major leagues. Even at 40, his legs scarred

by two decades of combat, Cobb could light up a ballpark with his intensity. Playing for the Athletics in 1927, he quickly quieted those who thought the spark was gone. He stole home on April 19 at Washington. A week later in Boston, he again stole home and then ended the game by racing in from right field to snare a line drive and then beating the runner who had been on first back to the bag for an unassisted double play.

T yrus Raymond Cobb was born in 1886 into a prominent family from Royston, Georgia. He was expected to go to college and become a surgeon. But from a very early age he demonstrated a talent for playing baseball that matched his love for the game, and by the time he was in his late teens, he was playing minor league ball. After a poor performance with Augusta in the South Atlantic League, he was released, and he later signed on with Anniston, Alabama, in the Tennessee-Alabama League.

But Cobb was determined to make it to the majors. So determined that, using a variety of handwriting styles and signing his name "Jones" or "Smith," he sent a number of letters to sportswriter Grantland Rice praising a young ballplayer named Cobb. Rice was taken in by the puffery and wrote in the *Atlanta Journal* that "Over in Alabama there's a young fellow named Cobb who seems to be showing an unusual amount of talent." Only years later did Rice learn that Cobb, who was batting about .270 at the time, had sent the letters himself.

In the minor leagues, Cobb enjoyed a reputation as a speedster who always hustled, but some thought his judgment was poor. Herman "Germany" Schaefer, the Tigers' second baseman, saw him play during spring training in 1905 and reported that he tried to steal a base on every pitch, tried to

Cobb's hands-apart grip helped make him one of the game's greatest bunters. And for him, the bunt was a true weapon. Hub Leonard once brushed him back, so on the next pitch Cobb bunted toward first base. Leonard took the throw and fled from the bag, but Cobb spiked him from behind.

In 1921 Cobb was elevated to player-manager, and while the Tigers had loads of talent, they never won a pennant under him. His six-year managing totals include a .519 winning percentage, one second- and two third-place finishes. The added duties didn't seem to bother his hitting; Cobb hit .365 as a player-manager, just two points under his lifetime average.

take two bases on singles and tried to go from first to third on bunts. "He's the craziest ballplayer I ever saw," Schaefer said.

Cobb failed to make the Tigers that spring, and returned to Augusta. The team lacked discipline, and Cobb soon began to lose his own ambition. The situation got so bad that he missed a fly ball in the outfield because he was busy eating a bag of popcorn. This angered Augusta's manager, George Leidy, but rather than give up on the disillusioned young player, Leidy took him under his wing. Leidy spent mornings before games teaching Cobb the ins and outs of the hit-and-run, the delayed steal, hitting to the opposite field and bunting. "Hour after hour Leidy threw to him and Cobb bunted at an old sweater placed to either side of homeplate," writes Cobb biographer Charles Alexander. "He worked on sacrifice bunts, on drag bunts, on faking bunts and slapping the ball past third basemen. And in the games in the afternoon, Leidy let Cobb do what he wanted at bat and on the basepaths, confident that with what he had learned, the kid would usually do the right thing."

Soon Cobb was the league's top player, earning $125 a month and expecting a call to join the Tigers. But in August 1905, he received a telegram informing him that his father had been shot to death. The elder Cobb, returning unexpectedly from out of town in the middle of the night, had attempted to enter his locked house through a window and was shot by his wife. Mrs. Cobb, who was rumored to have been carrying on an adulterous affair, was eventually exonerated. A month after the incident, Ty was called up to the Detroit Tigers and instantly became the butt of dugout sniping, which only chafed his already testy nature. The older players on the team resented Cobb's brashness, so they abused him some more; Cobb's inability to take their challenges good naturedly brought still more abuse. He one day entered

the Tigers' clubhouse to find the crown ripped out of his cap and his bats sawed in half. Even in later years, Cobb remembered the series of incidents with bitterness: "If I became a snarling wildcat, it was their fault. . . . It was the most miserable and humiliating experience I've ever been through." Sam Crawford, who regularly hit behind Cobb in the Tiger lineup, saw the situation from another angle: "He was still fighting the Civil War, and as far as he was concerned we were all damn Yankees. But who knows, if he hadn't had that terrible persecution complex, he never would've been about the best ball player who ever lived."

Bobby Veach (above, sliding) played alongside Cobb in the Tiger outfield for 11 full seasons and, with some instruction from Cobb, became one of the AL's most dangerous hitters. He led the league in RBI three times, and from 1913 to 1923 averaged 17 stolen bases a season.

Inside baseball—a heavily strategic game that was based on speed and aggressiveness—was in its heyday when Cobb joined the Tigers, and he was impressed by the caliber of major league play. "Such speed, class, style, speedy maneuvering, lightning thinking. . . . And they went at it with a red-eyed determination I couldn't believe," Cobb later wrote. Less than a week into his big league career, Cobb was initiated into the ways of this new world. Attempting a headfirst slide on a steal of second base, he was tagged out by the New York Highlander's Kid Elberfeld, who gratuitously stuck his knee into Cobb's neck and ground his face into the dirt. Sliding headfirst was at the time considered "bush league." Jeered by his teammates and manager, Cobb slid feetfirst the rest of his career.

Cobb made a number of rookie mistakes in the 41 games he played at the close of the 1905 season—more than once he ran the Tigers right out of a rally. But by the middle of 1906 he had become a highly regarded major leaguer, leading off and playing center field regularly. He was more comfortable on the field than off; he made few friends among his teammates and carried on a run-

Continued on page 50

Stealing Home

t may be the most exciting play in baseball; it's certainly the riskiest. A runner on third base cautiously leads off, then—as the catcher sets for the pitch, the batter readies himself, and the pitcher enters his windup—the runner sprints for home. Seeing the runner out of the corner of his eye, the pitcher hurries his throw. The batter tries to help the runner by blocking the catcher's view until the last second, while the catcher leaps out to grab the pitch and slap on the tag. The runner who finds the plate in the midst of all this chaos becomes a hero.

Steals of home are extremely rare today. Ty Cobb's lifetime record of 50 regular-season steals of home may last longer than any of the other marks he set. Rickey Henderson stole home only four times in his first ten years in the majors, while Vince Coleman has tried only twice and made it once in his first four years. By contrast, Lou Gehrig stole home 15 times, and even Babe Ruth did it ten times.

There are several reasons why stealing home has all but disappeared in today's game. First, in the low-scoring, dead-ball days when Cobb played, a stolen run was a better gamble because it could often mean the difference between a win and a loss. Second, in these days of big contracts, some players are reluctant to put their bodies on the line by risking a collision at home for a single run.

But the main reason is that teams are doing a better job of defending against the steal of home than they were 50 or 60 years ago. Third basemen now play closer to the bag and pay more attention to a potential base-stealer, preventing the leadoff needed to have a good chance. And most pitchers no longer take a big windup with a runner on third the way they did in earlier years. Nowadays, they generally check the runner as they move into the stretch position of their delivery. The stretch keeps the runner closer to third, and the pitcher needs less time to deliver the ball to the plate.

The most recent ballplayer to earn a reputation for stealing home was Rod Carew. Of Carew's 353 lifetime steals, 17 were of home. In 1969 he stole home seven times, equaling the major league record set by the Brooklyn Dodgers' Pete Reiser in 1946. A surprising five of those seven steals came in the first inning. Conventional wisdom says that you should steal home only late in the game when it means the tying or go-ahead run. "Pitchers don't expect you to take a risk so early and kill off a potential rally," Carew said.

Brooklyn's Jackie Robinson stole home 19 times in his career, the most notable steal coming in the 1955 World Series against the Yankees. But perhaps the most momentous steal of home took place in the 1886 championship series between the St. Louis Browns of the American Association and the heavily favored Chicago White Stockings of the National League. The Browns had won three of the first five games. In the tenth inning of Game 6, with the score tied 3–3, Browns outfielder Curt Welch was on third base with one out. Welch danced up and down the baseline, driving White Stocking pitcher John Clarkson to distraction. Welch took off, and Clarkson, in his hurry to get the ball home, threw the ball over catcher King Kelly's head. Welch raced home and hit the dirt with the "$15,000 slide" to gain the winner-take-all pot the Browns clinched with the victory.

Stealing home makes the most sense with two outs and a weak batter at the plate, which is exactly when Cincinnati's Joe Morgan (below) tried it in 1975. Pitcher Gary Nolan was up, and Morgan scored on the front end of a triple steal. Brooklyn's Jackie Robinson (left) chose Game 1 of the 1955 World Series for a high-profile dash homeward. Frank Kellert was at bat, and Yogi Berra was catching for the Yankees. Robinson was safe, but the Dodgers lost the game, 6–5.

6' 1" 200 lbs.   b 2/25/1884
BB TL   d 11/29/1942

BOB BESCHER
Outfield

In 1909, 25-year-old Bob Bescher stole a league-leading 54 bases for the Cincinnati Reds. It was the first of his four straight NL stolen-base titles, which included a career high of 81 in 1911. If Bescher's feats went largely unnoticed, it was partly because the Reds were a mediocre team and partly because the sports press was busy deifying AL speedster Ty Cobb.

After leaving the Reds in 1913, Bescher played one year with the Giants, three with St. Louis and one with Cleveland. He was only adequate as a hitter, with a .258 average. But once he got to first base, Bescher—not Cobb—was the most efficient basestealer in baseball. From 1909 through 1911, Cobb averaged 220 hits and 75 stolen bases a season. During the same time period, Bescher averaged 68 stolen bases on just 140 hits a season.

Bescher didn't intimidate opponents with his style of running but relied on sheer speed, surgical precision and careful study of a pitcher's motion. A master of the fall-away slide—a sudden drop to the ground just before reaching the base—Bescher always came in feet first and used one of two basic attacks, depending on the catcher's throw. "If it is high," he said, "I always slide for the inside of the bag; if it is low, I always slide for the outside." Bescher not only made it sound easy, he made it look easy. In just 11 years he stole 428 bases to place 24th on the all-time list.

Cleveland catcher Harry Bemis had a lackluster nine-year career in the majors, the sole highlight coming when he pounded Ty Cobb on the head with a baseball after Cobb had knocked him down on a play at the plate, jarring the ball out of Bemis' glove.

ning feud with outfielder Matty McIntyre. On the road he kept to himself, frequenting museums, art galleries and libraries, where he studied everything from Roman history to phrenology.

But he also spent much of his time trying to improve his skills as a ballplayer. Cobb decided that he had to charge balls hit on the ground rather than wait for them. He figured that he could get more momentum behind his throws if he ran up to catch fly balls instead of waiting under them. He also figured out that, as a baserunner, if he watched the eyes of the third baseman awaiting a throw from an outfielder and twisted his body accordingly, he could get in the path of the ball and deflect it with his back and perhaps score. He realized, too—Germany Schaefer's opinion notwithstanding—that there were times when he could advance from first to third on a sacrifice bunt. Once on base, he often signaled whoever followed him in the batting order to bunt. Cobb would then take off with the pitch and head around second to third.

Cobb and teammate Crawford were not on the best of terms personally, but Crawford marveled at Cobb's baseball sense. "It wasn't that he was so fast on his feet," Crawford remembered years later. "There were others who were faster. . . . It was that Cobb was so fast in his thinking. He didn't outhit the opposition and he didn't outrun them. He outthought them!" After running hard to reach base, Cobb would sometimes hold his leg and limp in order to fool the other team into thinking he was hurt; then on the next pitch, he'd race off at full speed on a steal. To increase his lead off first, he might kick the bag forward, taking advantage of the few inches of give in the strap. When he took his lead, he typically waved his arms, yelled at the pitcher and lunged ahead on false starts to upset the opposing ballclub.

TY COBB BOBBY VEACH SAM CRAWFORD

Stories of Cobb's baserunning exploits abound. Someone once described his style as "daring to the point of dementia." He was one of the few runners ever to cross up the New York Highlanders' Hal Chase, considered by many to be the finest fielding first baseman of the day. After taking a throw at first base with a runner advancing to third, Chase often threw the ball to third in hopes of catching the runner off base. In a 1907 game, Cobb doubled; on the next batter's sacrifice bunt, instead of stopping at third, he steamed for home. Chase, intending to throw behind Cobb, was befuddled. He tried to stop his throw to third but the ball went flying over the third baseman's head as Cobb scored. "It was maybe the graceful Chase's most embarrassing moment on the diamond in his fifteen years in the majors," according to Alexander. But it was typical Cobb; he regularly grabbed the advantage by anticipating what the opposition would do—by being one step ahead of the infielders, both physically and mentally.

Nor was Cobb above gaining the advantage in other, less cerebral, ways. In a game against Cleveland that same season, Cobb hit what should have been a triple to left center, but instead of stopping at third, he kept going as the third baseman relayed the throw home. Indians catcher Harry Bemis had the ball well before Cobb arrived, but Cobb lunged at him, knocking Bemis over and making him drop the ball. Bemis was so mad that he banged the sprawled out Cobb on the head with the ball until the umpire pulled him away. Undaunted, in his next two at-bats Cobb beat out a bunt, and then doubled and stole third.

In the ninth inning of Game 3 of the 1908 World Series against the Cubs, the Tigers held an 8–3 lead. Cobb notched his fourth hit and yelled to catcher Johnny Kling that he was going to steal second on the next pitch. He made

In 1915 the Tiger outfield of Ty Cobb, Bobby Veach and Sam Crawford finished 1–2–3 in the AL in RBI, hits and total bases. Cobb won the batting and stolen-base titles, while Crawford led the league in triples and Veach led in doubles.

Ruth on the Run

Babe Ruth: the name is synonymous with power. But despite the potbelly and extra pounds he carried late in his career, Ruth was fast. He raced around the basepaths for a career total of ten inside-the-park homers, and he stole home ten times. As a Yankee in 1923, he surprised his old teammates, the Boston Red Sox, by circling the bases for inside-the-park homers two days in a row.

INSIDE-THE-PARK HOME RUNS

Date	Opponents	Stadium
Apr. 23, 1919	New York Yankees	Polo Grounds
Aug. 11, 1923	Detroit Tigers	Yankee Stadium (2nd game)
Sept. 9, 1923	Boston Red Sox	Yankee Stadium (2nd game)
Sept. 10, 1923	Boston Red Sox	Yankee Stadium
Oct. 5, 1923	Philadelphia Athletics	Yankee Stadium
July 20, 1924	Cleveland Indians	Yankee Stadium (2nd game)
Aug. 25, 1924	Cleveland Indians	Yankee Stadium
Sept. 19, 1926	Cleveland Indians	League Park
July 8, 1927	Detroit Tigers	Navin Field (2nd game)
July 15, 1929	Detroit Tigers	Navin Field

STEALS OF HOME

Date	Opponents	Stadium
Aug. 24, 1918	St. Louis Browns	Fenway Park
June 4, 1920	Philadelphia Athletics	Yankee Stadium
Sept. 6, 1920	Philadelphia Athletics	Yankee Stadium (2nd game)
July 20, 1921	Cleveland Indians	League Park
May 1, 1923	Washington Senators	Griffith Stadium
July 28, 1924	Chicago White Sox	Comiskey Park (2nd game)
July 22, 1926	Chicago White Sox	Yankee Stadium
June 9, 1927	Chicago White Sox	Yankee Stadium
May 25, 1929	Boston Red Sox	Fenway Park (2nd game)
July 27, 1931	Chicago White Sox	Yankee Stadium (2nd game)

Chart information was supplied by L. Robert Davids

Indian outfielder Elmer Flick led the AL in steals in 1904 and 1906, then came in second to Cobb in 1907. After the 1907 season, Detroit offered to trade Cobb for Flick, largely because they thought Cobb's aggressive baserunning would shorten his career. Cleveland turned down the offer, and in 1908 Flick came down with a mysterious stomach ailment that effectively ended his career.

good his word, knocking over Chicago shortstop Joe Tinker in the process. Cobb then yelled that he was going to steal third on the next pitch and again was successful when Kling threw low. The Tiger batter, Claude Rossman, then walked, and in a rehearsed play, rounded first and started trotting toward second. Cobb sprinted for home, but was thrown out. It really didn't matter; he had delivered the message that he was willing to take any base at any time. He did steal home in the 1909 World Series, and he stole home a record 50 times during regular-season play.

Umpire Billy Evans remembered Ty Cobb as one of the best base-runners he had ever seen and was most impressed by Cobb's skill at sliding. Evans interviewed Cobb for an article called "Speed and the Base-Runner" in *St. Nicholas Magazine* in 1915. Cobb's remarks on sliding are a remarkable commentary on his scientific approach to the game of baseball:

"As I near a base, I make it a point to study carefully the position assumed by the man about to take the throw. From the position of this fielder, it is possible to get a pretty good line on what kind of throw has been made. If the fielder is in front of the bag, it becomes the duty of the runner to slide behind him, that is to throw in the foot as you near the bag, but twist the body in the direction of the outfield. This gives him only the foot to touch. If the fielder is taking the throw standing in the rear of the bag, hooking the foot in and throwing the body in the direction of the infield. The quicker the slide, the more difficult the touch. I make it a point to run almost on top of the base-man before hitting the dirt, and giving the body a twist to drive me away from the base-man.

Cobb played more games—and committed more errors—in the outfield than anyone else in the history of the American League. But when he wanted to, he could play the field and throw with the best of them, and with 392 assists, he ranks second all time behind Tris Speaker.

Outfielder Dode Paskert stole 293 bases from 1907 to 1921, but his fastest work came when he rescued 15 children from a burning building in Cleveland in 1920. Carrying the children out one by one, Paskert was severely burned but recovered in time to play 139 games that season.

"The player must not forget, too, that there is a difference between base-running and mere stealing of bases. Conditions of the game must always be considered, and good base-running often makes it imperative that the hit and run be used, when the theft of a base might make the player's record look better."

But Cobb was not universally admired. Whether stealing home or taking an extra base, Cobb usually came in with spikes high. Understandably, opponents were less than enchanted by such tactics. In 1909, after Cobb spiked Athletics third baseman Frank Baker and drew blood, the normally docile Connie Mack called Cobb the dirtiest player in the history of baseball. American League President Ban Johnson, who was not normally pacific, issued the Tigers an ultimatum: Cobb "must stop this sort of playing or he will have to quit the game." Johnson later recanted, acknowledging that the umpires present had not felt Cobb violated any rules.

While it is true that Cobb often injured opponents with his spikes, the stories that he sharpened his spikes to intimidate the opposition are doubtful. Tiger Sam Crawford said it wasn't so. Most likely, this story dates back to a 1908 incident in which a few Tigers bench-warmers did file their spikes to frighten the Highlanders. Still, there is no doubt that Cobb's success on the basepaths had as much to do with intimidation as it did with speed.

When Cobb became manager of the Detroit Tigers in 1921, he tried to create a team in his own image. Despite the unprecedented numbers of home runs being hit as the game entered the lively-ball era, Cobb continued to school his players in the fundamentals of inside baseball: bunting, the hit-and-run and baserunning. But this was the age of Babe Ruth, and the lessons

5' 11" 179 lbs.   b 8/6/1884
BR TR   d 3/13/1929

SHERRY MAGEE

Outfield

Even in the era of the dead ball, Sherwood "Sherry" Magee racked up some lively numbers. During his 16 years in the majors from 1904 to 1919, Magee led the National League in RBI four times and in slugging percentage twice, despite never having hit more than 15 home runs in one season.

But he was a slugger. In 1910 Magee's .331 batting average, .507 slugging average, 110 runs scored and 123 RBI topped the league. And in 1914 he led the league in hits, doubles, RBI and slugging average. In addition, he was a fine fielder, and in 1911 his .981 fielding average was the highest for outfielders.

Magee also earned a reputation for speed and cunning on the basepaths. In his first six full seasons with the Philadelphia Phillies, Magee averaged 46 stolen bases a year with a career high of 55 in 1906.

Magee was quick with his fists, too. In a game against St. Louis on July 10, 1911, he knocked out umpire William Finneran with a single punch after Finneran ejected him for disputing a called third strike.

Magee retired from the majors with 2,169 hits, a .291 batting average and 441 stolen bases. But he was far from through with baseball; he played for a host of minor league teams until 1926, and in 1928 he returned to the majors as an NL umpire. Magee quickly gained respect as a rookie umpire that year, but he contracted pneumonia and died before the start of the 1929 season.

In most confrontations between pitchers and hitters, the pitcher does most of the intimidating. Not so with hitters like Cobb. "Every great batter works on the theory that the pitcher is more afraid of him than he is of the pitcher," Cobb said.

were often lost on young men who dreamed of rounding all the bases at once, rather than advancing one base at a time.

Cobb's attitude toward Ruth was contemptuous. Their rivalry was built not only on the natural competition of two stars playing in the same league. It was also built upon their radically different approaches to the game. Cobb realized that Ruth's style of play, based largely and simply on power, was popular and posed a threat to his own brand of baseball.

It wasn't only Ruth's style of play that Cobb disdained, but also his happy-go-lucky love of life. Cobb believed that a player must dedicate himself year-round to the pursuit of excellence. While Ruth was drinking and womanizing during the off-season—and during the season itself, for that matter—and reporting to spring training out of shape, Cobb was leading a spartan life. Cobb's criticism of the colorful home run king was unrelenting and cruel. Focusing on the slugger's well-known lack of attention to personal hygiene, Cobb would wait for Ruth to pass by and then ask those around the batting cage if they smelled anything unusual. Cobb also used racial epithets to refer to Ruth because of his dark complexion. So the two became enemies as well as rivals, and there was tension whenever the Yankees met the Tigers.

A five-game Tigers-Yankees series at the Polo Grounds in June of 1921 not only played up the rivalry, but also foreshadowed the future. The first day of the series, Ruth homered. The second day, he homered and pitched the Yankees to victory. The Yankees swept the series, with Ruth blasting seven home runs. It was as if the young slugger were nailing shut the coffin of the dead-ball style of baseball that Cobb had championed.

Off the field, Cobb got into more than his share of scrapes. There were charges that Cobb, Cleveland manager Tris Speaker and his pitcher-

turned-utility outfielder, Smoky Joe Wood, had bet on a Tigers-Indians game in 1919; Speaker had apparently assured Cobb that Detroit would win. The charge that Cobb had bet on a fixed game was made in 1926 by former Detroit pitcher Dutch Leonard, another of Cobb's enemies. The accusation did appear to have merit, and AL President Ban Johnson banned Cobb from the league. But the allegations could not be proved conclusively, and Cobb was reinstated by Commissioner Kenesaw Mountain Landis.

Fortunately, the incident is but a footnote to the Cobb legend. More than 60 years after playing his last game, Cobb still holds baseball's highest lifetime batting average at .367 and is first in runs scored with 2,245. Cobb ranked first with 4,191 hits until Pete Rose passed him in 1985, and first in steals with 892 until Lou Brock passed him in 1977. He also ranks second to teammate Sam Crawford in triples with 297. He led the AL in batting a record 12 seasons, and took the Triple Crown in 1909 with a .377 average, nine home runs and 107 RBI. By today's standards he was anything but a slugger, but he led the AL for eight dead-ball seasons in slugging percentage. Perhaps equally important, he defined an entire era of baseball with his no-holds-barred style of play. In pre-World War I America, baseball was to Cobb a war and a way of life.

St. Louis Browns third baseman Jimmy Austin remembered an incident that defines the Cobb style perhaps better than any other. In a game against the Browns, Cobb was trying to go from first to third on a single, but as Cobb reached third, Austin pushed his foot off the base and tagged him. "Well, the umpire called Ty out," Austin recalled. "Ty didn't move a muscle. Just lay there on the ground. Then he looked up at me, and in that Southern brogue of his he said very slowly, 'Mister, don't you ever dare do that no more.' " ◑

Tiger owner Frank Navin (above, left) haggled annually in contract negotiations with Cobb. In 1913 Navin suspended Cobb for refusing to sign his contract, but when the publicity led to threats of a congressional investigation into baseball's labor practices, Navin quickly shifted his position and compromised.

Jimmy Sheckard

Ring Lardner said he was "the greatest ballplayer in the world." Grantland Rice claimed that he "deserved a place among the game's greatest outfielders." And Bill James wrote, "In his best years he was an awesome performer." Who's the object of all this praise? Does the name Jimmy Sheckard ring a bell? Probably not, for Sheckard, a brilliant left fielder who played for five National League clubs from 1897 to 1913, has been largely forgotten. His accomplishments, however, live on in the record books.

Jimmy Sheckard could do it all. Over his 17-year career, he led the NL 16 times in offensive and defensive categories, including stolen bases, home runs, slugging average, triples, runs, walks, assists, double plays and putouts. More than 75 years after he retired, he still ranks in the top ten in two categories: fifth in double plays by an outfielder and eighth in assists by an outfielder. And he's 11th on the all-time list in steals of home with 18.

The 5′ 9″, 175-pound Pennsylvania native was known for his keen eyesight and ability to wait for just the right pitch. In 1911 he set a league record with 147 walks; the mark stood for 34 years. His intelligent batting earned him the title "the premier base-on-balls man of his era," and his tremendous speed made him a constant base-stealing threat. He led the league in stolen bases in 1899 with 77 and in 1903 with 67.

Sheckard broke into the majors with the Brooklyn Dodgers in 1897 and bounced back and forth between the Dodgers and the Baltimore Orioles before he was traded—for *four* players *plus* $2,000 cash—to the Chicago Cubs in 1905. "Ole Jim," as his teammates called him, proved to be immensely popular with Cubs fans. In the dead-ball era, Sheckard's "live-wire" style of play—waiting out pitchers, stealing bases, trapping runners with his accurate arm —helped the Cubs snag four pennants and two World Series titles in five years. As one writer noted, "The wily outfielder played an aggressive, devil-may-care brand of ball, blending guts, determination and mental alertness into a team-oriented, selfless style of play."

After Sheckard joined Chicago, it seemed as if the Cubs could do no wrong. During his first year, they won 116 games and lost only 36 for a .763 winning percentage that has not been equaled since—and probably never will be. For the seven years that Sheckard was with the Cubs, they won two-thirds of their games. In spite of Sheckard's all-round skills, much of the recognition for the Cubs' success went to his better-known teammates, especially the famous infield trio of Tinker, Evers and Chance. Nevertheless, Bill James wrote that Sheckard "was certainly a greater player than Frank Chance and arguably greater than Tinker, Evers or anyone else on those teams except [pitcher Three Finger] Brown."

In 1913 the 34-year-old veteran ended his major league playing career by splitting the season between St. Louis and Cincinnati. Although he had lost much of his power and speed, he still had a keen eye and a quick mind. While he hit only .194 in his last season, he had an on-base percentage of .366.

Sheckard, the star who had earned as much as $4,300 a season, lost his savings in the crash of 1929 and ended his days as a gas station attendant.

Outfielder Jimmy Sheckard was a spectacular if inconsistent ballplayer. In 1903 Sheckard hit .332 and led the NL with nine home runs and 67 stolen bases. In 1904 his numbers tumbled to .239, one homer and 21 steals.

JIMMY SHECKARD

Outfield
Brooklyn Dodgers/Superbas
  1897–1898, 1900–1901, 1902–1905
Baltimore Orioles (NL) 1899 (AL) 1902
Chicago Cubs 1906–1912
St. Louis Cardinals 1913
Cincinnati Reds 1913

GAMES	**2,121**
AT-BATS	**7,610**
BATTING AVERAGE	
Career	**.275**
Season High	**.353**
SLUGGING AVERAGE	
Career	**.380**
Season High	**.536**
HITS	
Career	**2,095**
Season High	**197**
DOUBLES	
Career	**356**
Season High	**31**
TRIPLES	
Career	**136**
Season High	**19**
HOME RUNS	
Career	**56**
Season High	**11**
RUNS BATTED IN	
Career	**813**
Season High	**104**
RUNS	
Career	**1,296**
Season High	**121**
STOLEN BASES	
Career	**465**
Season High	**77**
STOLEN-BASE TITLES, NL	
	1899, 1903
WORLD SERIES	**1906–08, 1910**

Cat and Mouse

THE BASE STEALER

Poised between going on and back, pulled
Both ways taut like a tightrope walker.
Fingertips pointing the opposites,
Now bouncing tiptoe like a dropped ball
Or a kid skipping rope, come on, come on,
Running a scattering of steps sidewise,
How he teeters, skitters, tingles, teases,
Taunts them, hovers like an ecstatic bird,
He's only flirting, crowd him, crowd him,
Delicate, delicate, delicate, delicate—now!

—Robert Francis

Not since Joe Morgan in the 1970s has a second baseman combined speed, power and defense like the Cubs' Ryne Sandberg. In his first eight seasons in the majors, Sandberg averaged 17 homers and 31 stolen bases, and won seven Gold Gloves.

When speedsters like Gary Pettis (preceding page) reach base, pitchers like Boston's Bob Stanley have to decide how much attention they deserve. Trying to keep them from getting too big a lead is important, but it can divert a pitcher's attention away from the hitter. The best base-stealers can turn diverting a pitcher's attention into an art form.

atting has always outclassed baserunning as the prime feature of baseball offense," wrote sportswriter F. C. Lane more than 60 years ago. "But of the two, base-stealing calls for the greater daring, the keener headwork. The baserunner is forever confronted with a prospect of limitless possibilities. The actions of a star base-stealer on first are a miniature drama in themselves." And drama it is. A ballpark comes alive when a Vince Coleman or Rickey Henderson reaches first and immediately sets his sights on second. The battle—between pitcher and runner, runner and catcher, manager and manager—is on, and the possibilities are rife: pitchout, pickoff, rundown, safe, caught stealing. The mere anticipation of a stolen base brings fans to the edges of their seats.

The successful steal not only can produce runs by moving runners into scoring position, but the mere threat of a steal forces the opposition to change its defense and pitching. To Joe Morgan, the Cincinnati Reds' great second baseman who retired in 1984 as the sixth leading base-stealer in history, the mere threat of a steal changes a game's whole dynamics. When a good base-stealer reaches first, Morgan says, "the infield gets jumpy, because it doesn't know what's going to happen. The hitter gains an advantage because the catcher calls for more fastballs so he'll have a better chance of throwing the runner out. And the pitcher has to divide his concentration between the batter and the man at first base." Base-stealing threats also open up holes for hitters, as infielders abandon their normal positions to protect against the steal; the more feared the base-stealer, the bigger the holes.

Playing in the friendly confines of Wrigley Field, the Chicago Cubs have historically favored slugging over running. As a result, the Cubs have pro-

duced a lot of excitement, many home runs and only two division titles since 1945. No one could guarantee that a different strategy would bring better results, but a look back at the Cubs' 1984 team, the first since 1945 to advance to postseason play, is revealing.

In 1983 the Cubs' 140 home runs were the highest in the National League East—only six behind the Dodgers' top mark—and they led the league in slugging average and fielding percentage. That same year the Cubs stole 84 bases, the lowest number in the NL: a full 40 fewer than the Pirates, who had the second-worst total. The team finished with a 71–91 record, second from the bottom in both the league and their division.

Lee Elia had managed the Cubs for most of the 1983 season, but by spring training 1984, Jim Frey was at the helm. Frey had guided the Kansas City Royals to a World Series appearance in 1980. Playing in a large new stadium with an artificial surface, the Royals had built their team with speed in mind. Although Royals Stadium dwarfs Wrigley Field, and although the Cubs play on natural grass, new manager Frey saw no reason to abandon the style of play that brought success to Kansas City. "My teams have always enjoyed having the image of being aggressive, and having that image has always had an effect on the opposition," he said.

Unfortunately, the team Frey inherited in Chicago was short on speed. General manager Dallas Green remedied that before Opening Day when he acquired Bobby Dernier, a fleet center fielder and base-stealer, from the Philadelphia Phillies. Frey named Dernier as his leadoff man, to hit in front of second baseman Ryne Sandberg. That season, Dernier stole 45 bases, and his daring was contagious. Sandberg stole 32, and the entire team compiled 154 steals—70 more than the previous season and fourth best in the league.

The ability to make correct, split-second decisions about whether to go or stay is what sets great base-stealers apart. Julio Cruz (above) had the touch, and in 1981 tied an AL record with 32 consecutive steals without getting thrown out.

Expert base-stealers are successful 80 percent of the time or better, so infielders are entitled to celebrate when they nail one. Yankee shortstop Wayne Tolleson (right) gave the clenched fist as second baseman Willie Randolph tagged out the Angels' Mark McLemore in 1988.

Base-stealers are always looking for an edge, be it psychological, physical or cosmetic. Convince them that a shoe polish can make them slide faster, and you might sell truckloads.

Chicago's batting average was virtually the same as in 1983, and the team hit four fewer homers, but the Cubs won 25 more games, finishing 96–65 and winning the division by 6½ games. Pitching was at least partially responsible for the performance, as Cubs hurlers allowed 61 fewer runs than they had in 1983. But Frey credited the club's success at stealing bases as a major factor in the turnaround.

Statistical analysts of the game have argued that the steal is an over-rated, overused ploy because it does not produce runs often enough to justify its risk. They have created new statistical categories, such as "stolen base runs," that measure the runs created beyond what a league-average base-stealing team might produce. "A man who steals two bases in three attempts is merely spinning his wheels in terms of value to his team," say John Thorn and Pete Palmer in *Total Baseball,* "and even a man who succeeds at an 80 percent clip will have to steal a lot of bases—about 65—to create just one win beyond average." Still, most fans love to see players steal. Says Frey, who is now the Cubs' general manager, "The computer people have no understanding of the psychological, the human element of the game. What they don't understand is that you're dealing with 24 individuals, most of whom like to play an aggressive game. Nobody likes to be known as a 'safety first' player."

In recent years, especially, the number of daredevils has risen, perhaps because of the increase in artificial-turf ballparks, where speed is king. In the late 1960s and early 1970s, when most of the artificial-turf stadiums were built, the upsurge in stolen bases was dramatic. Three teams showed marked increases in stolen bases during their first seasons in artificial-turf ballparks. St. Louis' output increased by 28 the year they laid down carpet in Busch Stadium; Cincinnati's increased by 36 when they entered Riverfront Stadium;

and Royals Stadium inspired Kansas City to steal 20 more bases than they had in Municipal Stadium. And the numbers over the past 20 years prove the increasing importance of base-stealing throughout the majors. In 1969 the 24 major league teams stole a total of 1,850 bases; in 1989, 26 teams stole 3,116 bases—an increase of more than 68 percent.

And as artificial turf seemed to speed up the game, the competition among individual base-stealers accelerated too. Ty Cobb's career mark of 892 steals in 24 seasons lasted one year short of a half century; the St. Louis Cardinals' Lou Brock surpassed it in 1977. Brock's record of 938 steals over 19 seasons may not last as long. Entering 1990, Oakland's Rickey Henderson—who set the single-season record of 130 in 1982—had already stolen 871 bases in just 11 years. The Cardinals' Vince Coleman—who stole more than 100 in each of his first three seasons—and the Montreal Expos' Tim Raines—the National League leader for each of his first four years before Coleman burst on the scene—may also mount serious challenges.

A serious baserunner has to back up an aggressive image with success. A great home run hitter sends the ball out of the park in one out of every 15 at-bats. A great hitter makes good on one of every three chances. But a base-stealer must beat the defense four out of every five tries to be considered great. Pittsburgh Pirates pitching coach Ray Miller says, "I'm not impressed by the guy who has 30 stolen bases by July but has been caught 15 times. . . . You take yourself out of too many innings." Morgan is even more demanding: "The great base-stealer should make it at least 80 percent of the time," he says. The illusion that runners like Henderson and Coleman create is to make it look easy.

In 1983 the Chicago White Sox won their first AL West title, and the speed of center fielder Rudy Law was a big reason why. Law set a team record with 77 steals, led the Sox with 95 runs scored and led AL outfielders with a .994 fielding percentage. He was caught stealing just 12 times.

Good Run, No Hit

For home run hitters, slugging percentage says more than batting average. For base-stealers, on-base percentage tells the story. Speedsters can pile up huge numbers of steals despite having mediocre to downright lousy batting averages. Some get a lot of walks, like Rickey Henderson in 1982; others steal almost every time they get on base, like Vince Coleman in 1986. Below is a collection of players who led their league in steals in spite of their limited hitting skills.

Player	Team	Year	BA		BB	OB %	SB	CS	SB%
V. Coleman	Cardinals	1986	.232		60	.302	107	14	.884
T. Harper	Pilots	1969	.235		95	.350	73	18	.802
O. Moreno	Pirates	1978	.235		81	.339	71	22	.763
B. Campaneris	Athletics	1972	.240		32	.277	52	14	.788
B. Bescher	Reds	1909	.240		56	.325	54	–	–
D. Lopes	Dodgers	1976	.241		56	.329	63	10	.863
B. Campaneris	Athletics	1967	.248		36	.290	55	16	.775
F. Taveras	Pirates	1977	.252		38	.301	70	18	.795
V. Coleman	Cardinals	1989	.254		50	.315	65	10	.867
R. Henderson	Athletics	1982	.267		116	.397	130	42	.756

It's all a matter of time—and timing. Starting at the beginning of the pitcher's motion, "the average pitch takes about 1.3 seconds to reach the catcher's glove," says Johnny Oates, a former big-league catcher who now coaches for the Baltimore Orioles. And from the time the catcher receives the ball, "the average throw to second base takes about 2.0 seconds. The best runners make it from first to second in about 3.05 or 3.1. You're going to have a tough time throwing them out, but you have to get the guys who get down there in 3.4."

In this game of beat the clock, the pitcher and catcher try to decrease the time it takes for the ball to go from the mound to the plate and back to second base, and to increase the time it takes the runner to move from first base to second. Some runners will take off when they think a breaking pitch is coming, figuring that it will take longer for a curve than a fastball to reach home plate.

While speed is obviously an important element of the stolen base, it alone does not determine whether the runner will win the battle. "You can be the fastest man in baseball but not be able to steal a base unless you can analyze the pitcher," says the Cards' Coleman.

The Expos' Raines agrees. "When I first came up, I relied on my speed. But now the pitchers have begun to do different things when I get on base. They change their pitching motion. They speed up their delivery to the plate. They throw to first more often. As a result I've been learning how to read pitchers. When I'm on base or in the dugout when someone else is on base, I study what the pitcher is doing."

Reading a pitcher means knowing whether he is going to pitch to the batter or throw to first base. "This is the key to base-stealing, making the

Continued on page 68

Twenty-one years after Lou Brock ignited the Cardinals to a pennant in his first season with the club, Vince Coleman (opposite) repeated the trick. Coleman was called up on April 17, 1985, as a temporary replacement for an injured outfielder. But the move became permanent when Coleman stole 110 bases and the Cards went on to win the NL pennant.

Davey Lopes

Some players win ballgames with superior physical skills—overwhelming power, split-second reflexes, dazzling speed. Davey Lopes, who once set a major league record by stealing 38 bases in a row without getting caught, won mostly on desire.

Lopes was born in 1946 in the ghetto of East Providence, Rhode Island, one of ten children. His father died when he was a child; his mother worked as a domestic to support the family. He might have been lost to drugs or crime, like many of his childhood friends, if not for the challenge and satisfaction he found playing baseball. He also found a surrogate father in a local high school coach who steered him toward an athletic scholarship at Washburn University in Topeka, Kansas.

Unprepared for Washburn's typical midwestern environment, Lopes almost quit in his freshman year, but he decided to tough it out because, as he said later, he was determined "not to give in to the ghetto." Lopes' play at Washburn began to attract the attention of major league teams, but many scouts dismissed him because he was "too small"—just 5′ 9″ and 170 pounds.

In 1968 the Los Angeles Dodgers took a chance on Lopes and made him their 26th pick in that year's college draft. He was pleased but also peeved; he felt he should have been picked higher. But before he could prove his case on the playing field, he had an education to finish; he didn't report to the Dodgers until he completed his undergraduate degree in 1969.

During his early years in the Dodgers' farm system, Lopes played in the shadow of more heralded prospects like third baseman Ron Cey and catcher Steve Yeager. But from the beginning he was a go-getter, a dirty-uniform competitor who did what he had to do to win. Even more than his speed, his aggressive baserunning style rattled opposing pitchers and catchers and ignited rallies. As a Dodger rookie in 1973, he not only won a job as starting second baseman and leadoff hitter, he won a rare vote of confidence from veteran manager Walter Alston, who gave him the green light to run virtually whenever he wanted.

Lopes responded by stealing 36 bases in 1973 and 59 in 1974, when the Dodgers won their first pennant in eight years. In 1975 he put together his record streak of 38 consecutive stolen bases without getting thrown out, on his way to a league-leading total of 77; he also scored 108 runs. The next year he topped the league again with 63 steals, beating out competition that included St. Louis' Lou Brock and Cincinnati's Joe Morgan.

From 1974 to 1981 the Dodgers were one of baseball's most successful teams, winning four pennants and a World Series. Lopes' role was to jump-start the offense. As Alston put it: "Davey is the key. His aggressiveness sets our mood. When he gets on base, we always have a good chance of scoring."

Lopes himself said that sheer speed on the basepaths was less important than knowing when to steal. He prided himself on always getting a good jump by anticipating the pitch. His knowledge of pitchers' motions was so complete that he was rarely picked off or thrown out trying to steal. In stealing 557 bases during his career—13th on the all-time list—he had a success rate of .830, higher than Brock, Morgan or Maury Wills.

DAVEY LOPES

Second Base, Outfield
Los Angeles Dodgers 1972–1981
Oakland Athletics 1982–1984
Chicago Cubs 1984–1986
Houston Astros 1986–1987

GAMES	**1,812**
AT-BATS	**6,354**
BATTING AVERAGE	
Career	**.263**
Season High	**.283**
SLUGGING AVERAGE	
Career	**.388**
Season High	**.464**
HITS	
Career	**1,671**
Season High	**163**
DOUBLES	
Career	**232**
Season High	**26**
TRIPLES	
Career	**50**
Season High	**7**
HOME RUNS	
Career	**155**
Season High	**28**
RUNS BATTED IN	
Career	**614**
Season High	**73**
RUNS	
Career	**1,023**
Season High	**109**
STOLEN BASES	
Career	**557**
Season High	**77**
STOLEN-BASE TITLES, NL	**1975, 1976**
WORLD SERIES	**1974, 1977, 1978, 1981**

Davey Lopes (top, leaping over the Yankees' Jerry Mumphrey) committed just one error in his first three World Series, but in 1981 he committed six. Still, the Dodgers beat New York in six games, and Lopes stole four bases to bring his lifetime World Series total to ten, third highest of all time behind Lou Brock and Eddie Collins.

The Pittsburgh Pirates, who'd stolen 180 bases during the 1979 regular season, didn't steal a base against the Orioles in the World Series. But they didn't need to, as Pirate hitters like Bill Madlock (above, center)—who stole 32 during the season—feasted on fastballs from pitchers like Mike Flanagan (left). The Pirates hit .323 as a team in their seven-game win.

pitcher commit himself to home before you've committed yourself to run," says Dave Nelson, who stole 187 bases over a ten-year career and went on to coach the Chicago White Sox on baserunning. "Otherwise, once you're committed and he isn't, he can throw to first and you're dead." Morgan makes it even simpler, saying, "You look for the green light that says 'go' or the red light that says 'don't go.'"

Of course, the smarter pitchers may try to add a yellow light that makes the runner too cautious to go without looking one more time, but Nelson believes that every pitcher eventually gives himself away. "Pitchers are creatures of habit," he says. "If you watch them long enough, you'll see a certain thing that tells you the pitcher is going to the plate. It's at that precise moment—when you know the pitcher can't throw to first—that you accelerate and head for second base." Jesse Jefferson, who pitched for several American League clubs between 1973 and 1981, is a case in point. "When Jesse was pitching for the Angels, I told my guys, 'Hey, you can steal on him,'" recalls Nelson. "He had fairly quick feet to first base, but he had this twitch in the right cheek of his behind. Every time you saw the twitch, it meant he was throwing home. He never threw to first base after he twitched. I'd tell my players to take off as soon as they saw the reflex action in the cheek."

When Nelson was coaching first base for the White Sox, he carried a stopwatch out to his station so that he could time an opposing pitcher's delivery and then signal the results back to his manager in the dugout. If Nelson flashed four fingers, for example, this meant a delivery time of 1.4 seconds. Knowing what the pitcher's normal delivery time is—many teams have such information in their scouting reports; the Mets keep it posted in the

In 1980, with San Diego, Jerry Mumphrey stole 52 bases—including 27 straight without being thrown out. But in his last three seasons in the majors—with the Cubs (above)—he stole just three bases, and the frustration showed.

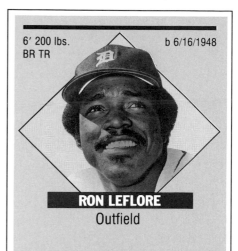

RON LEFLORE
Outfield

6' 200 lbs. BR TR   b 6/16/1948

dugout—the manager can tell whether the pitcher is slower or faster than average and then determine whether or not to send his runner.

Scouting reports also give a team information about when a team likes to steal and on what counts particular runners have a tendency to take off. Veteran catcher Jody Davis of the Atlanta Braves says two balls and one strike is the favorite count of many base-stealers. "The runner knows it's harder for us to pitch out then because we don't want to get further behind on the batter," he explains.

Many factors influence the decision to steal: the skills of the baserunner and the opposing battery, the score and inning, the number of outs and who's at the plate. And there are times when managers will signal a runner to remain at first rather than steal, holding the first baseman close to the line so that a left-handed hitter can take advantage of the hole between first and second. Managers also might forego opportunities to steal because they don't want the hitter to take pitches.

Just as the manager of the team at the plate may pass up a chance to steal, the manager of the team in the field may concede the stolen base. Miller says that he will often tell a pitcher not to worry about a runner, even in the later innings of a tight contest. "If you've got a guy who's pitching well, has maybe nine or ten strikeouts, let him go with his game and focus on the batter. Go with the odds that he can get the men at the plate out, and let the runner steal," he says.

Still, most pitchers feel compelled to keep at least one eye on the runner. And although savvy runners can learn to read hurlers, the man on the mound is not helpless. "There are things a pitcher can do," says Tom Seaver,

Speaking of his youth in Detroit, Ron LeFlore once said, "Stealing was my specialty." But he didn't mean base stealing. His specialty landed him in the state penitentiary at 19. It was there he played organized ball for the first time, and it was there the Detroit Tigers spotted him.

Only 11 months and 134 minor league games later, LeFlore was in the majors. He was as green as grass, but blessed with what one member of the Tiger front office called "the greatest raw tools" he'd ever seen. LeFlore hit a respectable .260 that year, but despite playing only 59 games, he managed to lead all AL outfielders in errors, and he struck out more than four times as often as he walked.

But LeFlore improved by leaps and bounds. He peaked in 1977, when he averaged .325 and got 212 hits. He led the AL in stolen bases in 1978 with 68, then bettered that with 78 stolen bases in 1979. He was traded to Montreal, where he stole 97 bases in 1980, leading the NL and becoming the only player to lead both leagues in stolen bases.

LeFlore closed out his major league career with the Chicago White Sox in October 1982, when he was suspended following his arrest on drugs and weapons charges. In just nine years in the majors he stole 455 bases, enough to rank 21st on the all-time list.

Southpaw John Tudor freezes baserunners by kicking his long right leg toward first, then delivering to the plate. But in 1985 Tudor didn't have many baserunners to worry about, as he went 21–8 for St. Louis with a 1.93 ERA and a league-leading ten shutouts.

Steve Carlton's pickoff move was one of the best in baseball, but umpires often found it to be illegal. Carlton led the NL in balks eight times, and in 1979 set a major league single-season record with 11.

who pitched in the majors for a remarkable 20 years. "Alter the delivery to home plate at different times to break the runner's timing. Avoid being repetitious. Maybe pitch out or throw a fastball to a location that helps the catcher if you think the runner is going. And, of course, periodically throw to first base to keep the runner close."

The typical pitcher has a variety of moves to first base. Bill Gullickson, who played for the Expos, Reds and Yankees before pitching in Japan, has three: "The first is just to show the runner I can come over there," he says. "The second is my deke; I try to make the runner think that's my best. And the third is my best. You always hold that until an important time in the game when you think you can actually pick someone off."

How does the first baseman know the pitcher is going to attempt to pick off a runner? Most teams employ a variety of plays. On one, the pitcher will signal the first baseman that he'll either throw to first or step off the rubber; under any circumstances, he won't throw home. On another, the catcher will initiate the pickoff by sending a signal to the pitcher. And on a third, the pitcher just throws to first when he sees daylight between the runner and first base.

This last move is not easy for the right-handed pitcher, whose back is to the runner and first base. Says Gullickson, "I can't actually see the runner. What I see is a shadow more than a moving figure, so I can't really see how far off the base he is. I judge that based on my throw to first. If he's just barely getting back, I get some feeling."

While the pitcher is measuring the runner, the runner is also measuring the pitcher. "Sometimes I try to make the pitcher give me his best move, so I can get a sense of how far to lead off," says Raines, who credits Fernando

Baltimore's Rick Dempsey was the hitting hero of the 1983 World Series, but he also did his usual fine job erasing base-stealers. Joe Morgan was the only Phillie who dared run on Dempsey, and the Oriole catcher threw him out twice in three attempts.

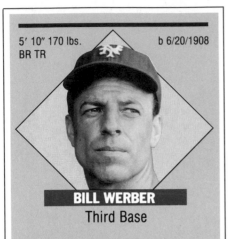

BILL WERBER
Third Base

In 1934, while headlines shouted about Detroit G-men, New York Giants and the Gashouse Gang, Bill Werber was quietly putting together the best season of his career. Laboring in obscurity for a .500 Red Sox team, the third baseman batted .321 and led the AL in stolen bases with 40.

He topped the league in steals again in 1935 with 29, and after being traded to the Philadelphia Athletics, he did it again in 1937 with 35. But despite his ability to make things happen on the field with his speed and his bat, Werber's shoulders were not wide enough to carry a whole team. Boston was never in a pennant race during his tenure, and the A's virtually owned last place.

In 1939 he was traded to Cincinnati, which he described as "a beautifully balanced team." No longer faced with the pressure to do everything, Werber became a model of consistency at third base. With the help of shortstop Billy Myers and second baseman Lonny Frey, he led the league in double plays with 34 in 1939, and in fielding percentage with .962 the following year.

By 1940 Werber had no more stolen base titles left in his legs—though his 16 was fourth best in the NL that season—but he still knew how to win. In the World Series that year his .370 average led all hitters as the Reds downed a tough Tiger team in seven games. Two seasons later, Werber played his last game with the New York Giants.

No one breathes in that split second between the tag and the umpire's call, but in 1980 Montreal's Rodney Scott rarely got a call he didn't like. Scott (above, with San Diego's Tim Flannery) stole 63 bases and was caught just 13 times.

Valenzuela and Steve Carlton with the best moves to first he has seen. To Vince Coleman, the toughest pickoff artists are the Phillies' Roger McDowell and Craig McMurtry, who pitched for the Braves before moving on to the Texas Rangers. But with pitchers he doesn't know, Coleman will sometimes draw the pickoff throw just to evaluate the pitcher's confidence. "I feel if he hasn't picked me off in four or five tries, he should leave it up to the catcher; that's his job. The pitcher's priority is to get the batter out. He had his chance with me when I was at the plate."

Large leads do not guarantee successful steals. Most of the top base-stealers take a lengthy 4½ step lead from first base, but Rickey Henderson's conservative lead leaves him a full step closer to first. Why is he so successful? According to former Angels' manager Gene Mauch, he more than compensates by getting the quickest start Mauch has ever seen.

"You have to get a quick start," says Morgan. Along with Raines and many other successful stealers, Morgan is a strong believer in the "crossover step," shooting the left leg—the one closest to first base—over and around the right foot, pivoting on the right and then flying. The technique gives the baserunner the same thrust a sprinter gets when coming up and out of the blocks.

Once the runner is in flight, the responsibility for bringing him back to earth rests solely with the catcher. The men behind the plate recognize they are at a disadvantage. "You'd like to get base-stealers out at a rate of about 50 percent, but 40 to 45 percent is more realistic. The percentage will be higher the more help the pitcher gives you," says Gary Carter, former Mets All-Star catcher.

Carter and other good catchers help the pitchers help them. Just as a batter adjusts his stance to fit a particular situation, a catcher changes his crouch when a base-stealer makes it to first, and his throwing hand, previously tucked safely behind the thigh, comes forward. "On every pitch I anticipate that the runner is going," says Carter. "I'm ready to throw."

When the bases are empty, a catcher's job is to keep the target low for the pitcher. When there are runners on base, the catcher has to be in position for instant action. This is particularly true if a left-handed hitter is up at bat, screening the catcher's view of the runner. Says Davis, "When a lefty is up, I have to rely on an infielder or the bench to tell me the runner is going."

When Davis started with the Cubs in 1981, his efforts at throwing out base-stealers were erratic at best. In 1984 the Cubs hired Johnny Oates—a highly regarded defensive catcher during his 11-year playing career—as a special tutor. Oates made quickness a priority: "Some catchers rely on arm strength, some on quickness, and some a combination of the two. There is a misconception that quickness means quick hands, getting hold of the ball and getting rid of it fast. That's important. But you have to start with the feet. If your feet are slow, it doesn't matter how fast your hands are because you'll be throwing with all arm and no body strength."

Adds Davis: "If my feet don't move, I usually don't make a good throw. I'm just like the infielder who tries to throw while standing flat-footed, and I may throw it over the infielder's head. But if I can get my feet going, the rest of my body and my hands just seem to automatically catch up."

Once a catcher masters the footwork, it's time to master the 130-foot throw. Oates counsels his catchers to hold a ball with fingers across the

Alan Wiggins stole 70 bases in the 1984 regular season, then kept on running in the World Series against Detroit. In Game 5 the Padre second baseman singled, stole second and went to third when catcher Lance Parrish's throw went into center field. But when Wiggins tried to score (above) on a bouncer to second, Lou Whitaker made a strong throw and Parrish tagged him out.

Rickey Henderson makes headlines by stealing bases, but he makes millions by scoring runs. In 1985 he scored 146 for the Yankees, the most since Ted Williams scored 150 in 1949. "My job is to score—score and win," Henderson says.

The loneliest spot on a baseball diamond is in the dust around second base after you've been caught stealing to end an inning. A potential rally has been killed, your uniform's a mess and it's a long walk to the dugout. Toronto's Nelson Liriano (opposite) got caught only twice in 15 attempts in 1987, but he took this one pretty hard.

seams for control, to the point that his charges instinctively reach for the seams, even in the locker room or on the bench.

When he worked with Davis in Chicago, Oates put the catcher through special agility drills and also pitted him against the clock. "When we pretended Jody was going not against the runner, but against the stopwatch, he became aware of quickness and the need for footwork," says Oates. The coach told Davis that the "magic number" to get the ball to second base was two seconds. Davis' throws to second were first clocked around 1.95 and 2.0 seconds, but by midseason, the time was down to between 1.7 and 1.8 seconds. "He even had a couple of 1.6s, fastest I've ever clocked," says Oates.

If the catcher's throw beats the runner to second base, the umpire will usually call the runner out, unless the defender is obviously late with the tag or misses it altogether. But Davis knows he can't depend on the umpire. "You're always looking for an advantage," he says. "Sometimes I'll look into our opponent's dugout between pitches and watch the manager. Maybe he won't do anything for three pitches and then you see him do something a little out of the ordinary and the guy steals on that pitch. So the next time you see the same sign, maybe you pitch out," Davis says. "It's one big guessing game." ◗▮

Luis Aparicio

Rarely has a mantle of greatness been passed more tenderly—or more directly—than it was on a ballfield in Maracaibo, Venezuela, in 1953. Luis Aparicio Sr. was, by all accounts, the greatest Venezuelan shortstop ever. Known as "the Great One of Maracaibo," Aparicio had been offered a contract by the Washington Senators in 1939 but turned it down. Still, he was a legend in Latin America, having played for 20 years in Mexico, Puerto Rico and Venezuela. But by 1953 Aparicio was 40 years old, his skills had declined, his team was in last place and his 19-year-old son, Luis Jr., was on the bench.

On November 18 Luis Sr. decided a change was in order. He played until he fielded his first ground ball of the game, then motioned toward the dugout for Luis Jr. to come out. The youngster trotted out to shortstop, where his father offered him a few words of advice, then handed him his glove. They embraced, then Luis Sr. took his son's place in the dugout and, according to one newspaper account, wept. Luis Jr. wasn't so sure. "I don't know whether my father cried," he said. "I was too nervous to cry. I went 0 for 4 and dropped a fly ball."

He didn't drop many after that. In fact, by the time his major league career was over, Luis Jr. had played more games, turned more double plays and thrown out more runners than any shortstop in history. And for nine straight years—longer than anyone else—he reigned as the American League's stolen-base king.

The pipeline from Venezuela to the hole between second and third at Chicago's Comiskey Park opened in 1950, when Chico Carrasquel took over from Luke Appling as the White Sox' shortstop. Carrasquel's uncle Alex—a pitcher with the Senators from 1939 to 1945—was the first Venezuelan to play in the majors, but Chico was the first shortstop. And he was a good one, leading the AL in fielding percentage three times in his first six years. But by 1955 the White Sox management decided Aparicio was better, so Carrasquel was traded to Cleveland for slugger Larry Doby. Aparicio opened the 1956 season as Chicago's starting shortstop and closed it as Rookie of the Year, getting 22 of a possible 24 votes. He hit a respectable .266 and led the league with 21 stolen bases, 250 putouts and 474 assists.

It was 1965 before anyone else led the AL in steals, and it was Aparicio's success—perhaps as much as anyone else's—that brought the running game back to baseball. Stealing bases wasn't in everyone's playbook in the late 1950s, and often Aparicio stole more bases in a season than did entire teams. In 1959 he stole 56 bases—more than every other AL team except the Red Sox—and led the Go Go Sox to the AL pennant.

Aparicio had outstanding natural speed, but it was his ability to slip quickly into high gear that made him such a great base-stealer. "He gets into high speed with one step," White Sox coach Tony Cuccinello said. Marty Marion, a fine shortstop in his own right and White Sox manager in 1956, watched Aparicio during his first game in a White Sox uniform and offered a more vivid description of his powers of acceleration. After seeing Aparicio score from second on a force-out, Marion said, "That kid runs like a scalded dog!"

Aparicio's great acceleration and timing allowed him to take a shorter lead than most base-stealers. Because he rarely had to worry about getting picked off, he could get his momentum going toward second, then abort his mission if the takeoff wasn't just right.

Luis Aparicio (below, with Yankee first baseman Moose Skowron) had the quickest acceleration in baseball in the 1960s. In 1960 he stole 51 bases in 59 attempts for an 86.4 percent success rate. "Even a good throw won't stop me once I get a good jump," he said.

After a five-year stint with Baltimore (opposite), Aparicio returned to the White Sox and had two of his finest years. In 1969 he hit a then-career-high .280 and stole 24 bases in 28 attempts, then followed it up with a .313 mark and a career-high 29 doubles in 1970.

Baltimore, where he and third baseman Brooks Robinson made the left side of the Oriole infield all but impenetrable.

Aparicio ate up ground in all directions at shortstop. Marion, who had been known as "Mr. Shortstop" in the 1940s, said, "I couldn't come close to fielding with Luis. Balls he flags down were past me before I could move." Billy Pierce, who pitched in the majors for 18 years, said, "I never saw anybody with Luis' instincts. He not only had great range, but he knew how to play the hitters." Aparicio won nine Gold Gloves by making plays that, according to White Sox owner Bill Veeck, "can't be made."

Aparicio finally played on a world champion with Baltimore in 1966, then in 1968 was traded back to the White Sox. The only knock on Aparicio throughout his career had been his hitting, but in 1970 he did something no one had expected: he hit .313, topping his previous career high by 33 points. He was asked to explain but couldn't. "I'm using the same bat, the same stance. I don't know the pitchers any better now, so I'll tell you the truth. It's one big mystery to me."

Aparicio retired after the 1973 season, taking with him a locker full of fielding and base-stealing records. Twelve years later the White Sox showcased yet another speedy, slick-fielding Venezuelan shortstop, Ozzie Guillen. By then, Aparicio was in the Hall of Fame. At just 5' 7" and 150 pounds, he proved to be the most durable shortstop in history and was a five-star general in the speed revolution that blitzed baseball in the 1960s. As for his glove, well, when author William Curran, a fielding aficionado for more than a half century, went to pick a shortstop for his all-time fielding team, the choice was clear. "I ran replays of half a dozen of my favorite shortstops past the inner eye, but my choice always returned to Luis," he said. "For speed, style and efficiency, I have seen none better."

"When I decide to go, I just go. If I don't get a good jump, I come right back to the base," he said. And Aparicio was as great a baserunner as he was a base-stealer. "I've seen lots of baseball in my days," said White Sox trainer Doc Froelich, "but the prettiest sight in the game is watching that guy go from second to home on a single."

As celebrated a base-stealer as Aparicio was, his quickness and great instincts earned even more accolades when they were displayed in the field. He was the league leader in assists as a rookie in 1956, and it wasn't until 1962 that he gave up the title. And in 1959 he began a record-tying string of eight consecutive years in which he led AL shortstops in fielding percentage. From 1956 to 1962, Aparicio and second baseman Nellie Fox—each with a cheekful of tobacco—formed one of the game's best double-play combinations. Then "Little Looie" was traded to

LUIS
APARICIO

Shortstop
Chicago White Sox 1956–1962
Baltimore Orioles 1963–1967
Chicago White Sox 1968–1970
Boston Red Sox 1971–1973
Hall of Fame 1984

GAMES	**2,599**
AT-BATS *(10th all time)*	**10,230**
BATTING AVERAGE	
Career	**.262**
Season High	**.313**
SLUGGING AVERAGE	
Career	**.343**
Season High	**.404**
HITS	
Career	**2,677**
Season High	**182**
DOUBLES	
Career	**394**
Season High	**29**
TRIPLES	
Career	**92**
Season High	**10**
HOME RUNS	
Career	**83**
Season High	**10**
RUNS BATTED IN	
Career	**791**
Season High	**61**
RUNS	
Career	**1,335**
Season High	**98**
STOLEN BASES	
Career	**506**
Season High	**57**
STOLEN-BASE TITLES, AL	**1956–64**
ROOKIE OF THE YEAR	**1956**
WORLD SERIES	**1959, 1966**

Little Napoleon and the White Rat

John McGraw practiced as a player what he later preached as a manager— find a way to get on base, then find a way to score. McGraw's lifetime on-base percentage was a lofty .460, and he scored .93 runs a game during his career with the Orioles, Cardinals and Giants.

John McGraw's Giants ran their way to three straight NL pennants in 1911, 1912 and 1913, and first baseman Fred Merkle (preceding page, being thrown out at home against Brooklyn) contributed his share. Merkle's 49 steals in 1911 were fourth best in the league, but only third best on his own team.

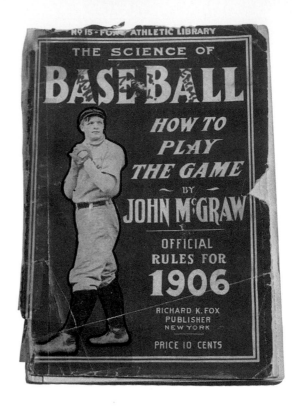

John McGraw's father had grown impatient with his son's passion for baseball. On several occasions, John's hits had broken neighbors' window panes, and each time, McGraw senior, already struggling to support his family, had to scrape together the 15 cents to pay for the damage. In the fall of 1885, when John was 12, his father paid a neighbor for another broken pane, and then turned on his son in a rage so terrible that John left home never to return.

He didn't go far; he took up residence in a boarding house across the street. And he did continue his love affair with baseball, although he altered his game. As a 16-year-old semipro who batted left, he became an expert at slicing hits to his left to avoid breaking the windows of a schoolhouse that sat in right field.

By the time he was 21, McGraw was leading off for Ned Hanlon's old Baltimore Orioles of the National League. The bat control McGraw had demonstrated in avoiding schoolhouse windows was never more apparent. Before 1901, foul balls did not count as strikes unless the umpire judged that the batter was intentionally hitting the ball foul. McGraw became a master at hitting "unintentional" fouls. Standing upright, his hands choked well up on the bat, and swinging with a chopping motion, McGraw fouled off pitch after pitch until an exasperated hurler either threw the ball where McGraw wanted it or walked him. According to Wee Willie Keeler, who followed McGraw in the Orioles' batting order: "There wasn't any of them that could foul 'em off harder than McGraw. He could slam 'em out so fast that even the umpire couldn't tell he was doing it on purpose."

Once he reached first base, McGraw flashed the hit-and-run sign to Keeler and took off with the pitch. Keeler then used his trademark "hit

'em where they ain't" tactic—punching the ball through the hole created when either the second baseman or the shortstop ran to cover second base. Rounding second base full steam ahead, McGraw could easily reach third base on the hit.

In addition to the hit-and-run, the Orioles popularized the "Baltimore Chop"—swinging down at the ball and hitting it toward third with such a high hop that a fleet-footed hitter could outrun the third baseman's throw to first. McGraw and teammate Hughie Jennings, who went on to an illustrious career as a manager, had the Orioles' groundskeeper pack the dirt hard around home plate to facilitate high bouncers.

Although John McGraw's inside baseball had its roots in Baltimore, it blossomed in New York when he became player-manager for the Giants in 1902. As baseball's dominant team for the next 20 years, McGraw's Giants featured fine pitching. But what separated the team from the rest of the pack year in and year out was its speed and aggressive play. In 1904, for example, the Giants captured the NL pennant by winning 106 games—then a major league record. That season, no one on the team hit .300, but the Giants—fast and feisty in their skipper's image—stole 283 bases.

How fast was McGraw himself? In 1894 the 5′ 7″, 155-pound third baseman stole 78 bases. How feisty? In spring training with the Orioles in 1893, McGraw, playing shortstop, held a Chattanooga runner by the belt to keep him from advancing on a fly ball, spiked an opposing player who was sliding into second base and slapped another sliding opponent in the face with the ball, giving him a bloody nose. When his career as player-manager ended

Between them, John McGraw (above, left) and Frank Chance managed all but one of the NL pennant-winning teams from 1904 to 1913. McGraw's Giants won five pennants during the span, while Chance's Cubs won four.

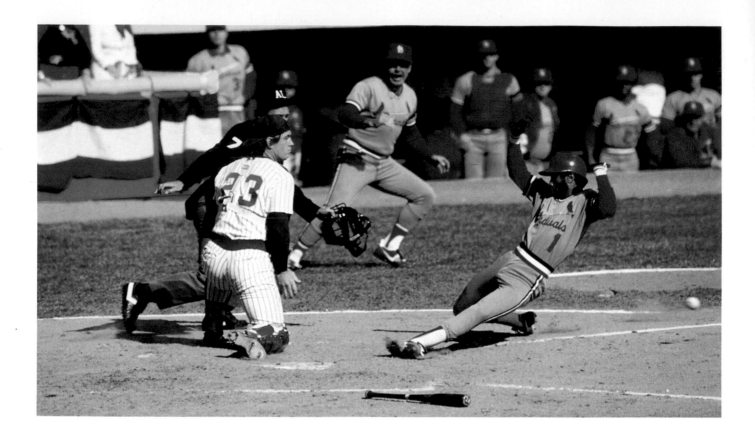

Manager Whitey Herzog (below) turned his Cardinals loose on the bases in 1982, and wound up getting lots of runs on not many hits. In Game 4 of the World Series against Milwaukee, St. Louis scored three runs in the second on just one hit, with two (including Ozzie Smith, above) scoring on a long sacrifice fly when Gorman Thomas slipped after making the catch.

and he became full-time manager of the Giants, he was rough on his players and even rougher on umpires. When manager McGraw coached at third base, he wore a fielder's glove in the coach's box. The Giants' fabled pitcher Christy Mathewson, who had a ghostwritten column in a New York paper, described what McGraw did when one of his men reached first base: "McGraw leaps in the air, kicks his heels together, claps his mitt, shouts at the umpire, runs in and pats the next batter on the back, and says something to the pitcher. . . . The whole atmosphere inside the park is changed in a minute."

Under McGraw, the Giants' offense was built around the hit-and-run and the stolen base, and no one but the pitcher could sacrifice bunt. "What's the use of having hitters if they can't advance the baserunner?" McGraw asked, referring to the hit-and-run.

McGraw's reliance on the running game reflected not only his personality, but his belief that teams had to manufacture more runs than they could get from swinging away. But in the years that McGraw managed the Giants, the way of playing baseball changed. With the introduction of the spitball and various rule changes—including a larger home plate and the rule making the first two foul balls strikes—pitching had assumed an increasingly dominant role. McGraw initially protested the foul-strike rule, enacted while he was still playing, since it seemed directed at him. He continued to argue against it when he became manager, believing that the rule put the hitter at a disadvantage and had taken the excitement out of the game. At the league meetings in December of 1904, he told reporters, "People do not care for ten- and eleven-inning games with a 1 to 0 score. They want action produced by clean, hard hitting and plenty of action in the shape of steals and runs."

McGraw's 1911 Giants had speed in both the bullpen and the dugout. Complementing a pitching staff led by Mathewson and Rube Marquard was a lineup of fast men and first-rate baserunners, five of whom stole 38 or more bases. Tops on the team was Josh DeVore with 61 steals. Fred Snodgrass had 51; Fred Merkle, 49; Red Murray, 48; and Larry Doyle, 38. In all, the Giants stole 347 bases, a modern-day, single-season record that still stands.

These players were all schooled in the McGraw method of baserunning. At spring training, the manager personally supervised sliding practice. Convinced that sliding headfirst ran a player directly into a tag, McGraw insisted on feetfirst slides—particularly the hook and the fall-away—which he believed got the runner to the base just as quickly and gave him a better chance of evading the tag.

McGraw's fleet-footed, hard-driving Giants won 105 games and the World Series in 1905, and then—after a drought of five years marked by three second-place finishes, one third-place and a fourth—the Giants won three straight pennants in 1911, 1912 and 1913. Acknowledged by the press and public alike as a managerial genius, McGraw was given the lion's share of the credit for the team's success. When the Giants took a series from the Cubs in 1911, Chicago's second baseman Johnny Evers said, "The Giants are a second-division team with a first-division manager. Without McGraw they wouldn't be heard of."

Although widely acclaimed as a manager without peer, McGraw did have his critics, who noted that his teams were not as successful in World Series play as might be expected, having won only three of the nine they played. Mathewson questioned his manager's reluctance to bunt runners into

Giants right fielder Red Murray (above, sliding) once disobeyed a McGraw order—and it cost him. With the winning run on second and none out, Murray was told to bunt, but instead swung away and hit a home run. After the game, McGraw fined him $100. But Murray usually played McGraw's game, and averaged 45 steals in the five full seasons he played with the Giants.

Continued on page 88

Royals Stadium

There's a singularity of purpose about Royals Stadium that no other stadium can match —and that purpose is baseball, pure and simple. No rock concerts, rodeos or religious revivals here, and if you want to see football you have to cross the parking lot to Arrowhead Stadium, where the NFL's Chiefs play.

Royals Stadium was designed exclusively for baseball, and it shows. Every seat points toward second base, and there isn't an obstructed view in the house. Instead of bleachers in center field—where white-shirted fans can make hitting a baseball like shooting polar bears in a blizzard—Royals Stadium substitutes a lush green lawn, providing one of baseball's best hitting backgrounds. It's easy to reach —just a stone's throw off Interstate 70—and easy to park—the lot has 16,000 spaces for a stadium that holds just 40,625 fans. And it's easy on the eyes, with a center field scoreboard that rises 12 stories above the playing field, providing a majestic backdrop for the largest privately funded water fountain display in the world.

The stadium itself was publicly funded. In 1967 Jackson County residents voted to authorize $43 million for construction of the Harry S. Truman Sports Complex. Six months later Kansas City was awarded its expansion franchise, but it wasn't until almost six years later that the stadium finally opened. It was worth the wait. As 39,464 fans looked on, the Royals christened their new stadium with a 12–1 win over Texas on April 10, 1973. Attendance almost doubled that season to 1,345,341, and the Royals finished second.

They finished second again in 1975, then in 1976 gave Kansas City its first major league title—the AL West crown. Infielders Cookie Rojas and Freddie Patek celebrated by jumping into the stadium's huge water fountain. Third baseman George Brett won his first batting title, and the Royals took advantage of their speed and that of the stadium's Tartan Turf surface to lead the AL in doubles and triples. They won AL West titles again in 1977 and 1978, and again led the league in doubles and triples. But the AL Championship Series had become a Bronx nightmare, as K.C. lost three straight times to the Yankees.

In 1980 the worm turned—at least halfway. Brett hit .390, and K.C. swept the Yankees in the ALCS but then fell to the Phillies in the World Series. In 1985 the Royals finally won it all, coming back from a 3–1 deficit in the ALCS to beat Toronto, then repeating the miracle in the Series against St. Louis, winning the last two games at home. It was a fitting conclusion, since the Royals have always felt right at home in Royals Stadium. In their six division-winning seasons, they combined for a .622 winning percentage at home, and Royals' teams traditionally feature speedy line-drive hitters, perfect for the stadium's quick turf and spacious power alleys. Designated hitter Hal McRae found the gaps for 54 doubles in 1977—the highest total since 1950—and a parade of fleet-footed outfielders like Amos Otis, Willie Wilson and Bo Jackson have plugged those same gaps for the home team.

Of the flurry of stadiums built in the 1970s, Royals is the shining star. Commissioner Bowie Kuhn called it "a miracle," author Bob Wood called it "a masterpiece" and even Reggie Jackson couldn't find anything wrong with it. "That stadium just gives you a lift," he said. "You really feel like playing when you get there."

New Home of the Kansas City Royals Baseball Club

Even if it isn't the game, there's always something interesting to watch at Kansas City's Royals Stadium. The stadium's scoreboard features a 40' x 60' video screen, and from center field to the right field corner is a series of water fountains, one of which rises and falls in response to the fans' cheers.

Royals Stadium

1 Royal Way,
Kansas City, Missouri

Built 1973

Kansas City Royals, AL
  1973-present

Seating Capacity
40,625

Style
Major league classic

Height of Outfield Fences
12 feet

Dugouts
Home: 1st base
Visitor: 3rd base

Bullpens
Home: right center field
Visitor: left center field

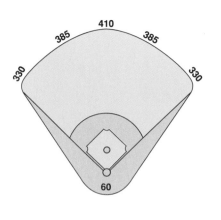

"Laughing Larry" Doyle was one of McGraw's slashing hitters who ran the bases as if they owned them. Doyle, a second baseman, had a whopping 25 triples in 1911 and stole home 17 times in his career. He played on three straight pennant-winners from 1911 to 1913, and in 1911 said, "It's great to be young and a Giant."

Outfielder Josh DeVore batted leadoff for the pennant-winning Giants in 1911 and 1912, and was one of McGraw's best jackrabbits. In a 21–12 Giants win on June 20, 1912, DeVore stole four bases in a single inning.

scoring position and suggested that because McGraw—nicknamed "Little Napoleon" for his dictatorial ways—controlled everything from the bench, his players could not improvise when it was important to do so, particularly in a short series.

Still, it seems fairer to blame those World Series losses on factors other than McGraw. His record during the lively-ball era shows just how good a manager he was. The Giants won NL pennants from 1921 to 1924, although the game was radically different from what it had been a decade earlier. In 1923 and 1924 the Giants had 106 and 82 steals, respectively—less than one-third as many as they had compiled in 1911. McGraw showed that, like the best of managers, he could adapt his strategies to the changes in the game itself. "With the . . . ball being hit all about the lot," he said, "the necessity of taking chances on the bases has decreased. A manager would look foolish not to play the game as it is, meet the new situation with new tactics. . . . There is no use of sending men down on a long chance of stealing a bag when there is a better chance of the batter hitting one for two bases, or, maybe, out of the lot." But like Ty Cobb, McGraw was a reluctant participant in such slugging matches, and he acknowledged that he missed "the thrill . . . of seeing men shoot down the basepaths, one after another until they had stolen their way to a win. That was baseball—the kind of baseball that I learned when I got my first job." By the time he retired in 1932, McGraw had become disenchanted with the new game. "Nowadays, the game has become a case of burlesque slugging, with most of the players trying to knock home runs." Bemoaning the absence of scientific baseball, he proposed shortening the pitching distance to 58 feet to encourage a greater

balance between pitching and hitting. But no one listened. The rest of the baseball world was swept up in the excitement over the long ball.

Whitey Herzog was only six months old when John McGraw ended his 33-year career as a manager. But while they played and managed in different eras and would never have been mistaken for each other on the basepaths, the two skippers are ideological twins. McGraw was the greatest practitioner of inside baseball—a game built on speed and strategy—in the early years of the century, before the home run became king. Herzog—along with Billy Martin—has been the leading proponent of inside baseball since the running game returned to baseball in the 1960s.

Herzog's first managerial job came with the Texas Rangers in 1973, a full ten years after he had ended an inauspicious eight-year major league career in which he played for four teams. Herzog's Rangers went 47–91 before he was fired and replaced by Martin. After managing four games in an interim capacity for the California Angels in 1974, Herzog became the skipper of the Kansas City Royals during the latter part of the 1975 season, taking over from Jack McKeon.

Built in 1973, Royals Stadium—with its long fences, deep power alleys and artificial turf—is typical of the modern-era ballpark, which rewards speed. Inheriting a team with such fast men as Amos Otis and Freddie Patek, Herzog immediately instituted his "run, boys, run" program. In 1976 seven Royals stole 20 or more bases—Patek topped the list with 51—and the team increased its stolen-base output from 155 to 218, second best in the league. The result was the team's first division title. Only a dramatic home run by the

Hall of Famer Ross Youngs did it all for the Giants from 1918 to 1926. He hit .322 and averaged 26 doubles, 10 triples and 17 steals a year. And he was just as good in the field, leading the NL in assists three times. After the 1925 season, Youngs was stricken with kidney disease, and in 1927 the man McGraw called "my greatest outfielder" died at the age of 30.

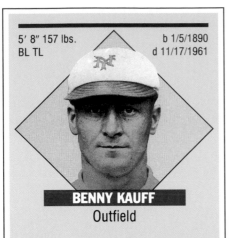

5′ 8″ 157 lbs.
BL TL

b 1/5/1890
d 11/17/1961

BENNY KAUFF
Outfield

He was called the "Ty Cobb of the Federal League." Benny Kauff, a fun-loving character from the Ohio coal fields, was famous for wearing diamond rings and silk underwear—and for hitting and running. In 1914, his first full season in the majors, he was the Federal League's top hitter with a .370 average and its top base-stealer with 75. Those numbers helped his team, the Indianapolis Hoosiers, finish first. In 1915 Kauff signed with the Brooklyn Federals for $6,000—a $2,000 raise—and again led the league with a .342 average and 55 stolen bases.

Such numbers caught the eye of Giant manager John McGraw. When the short-lived Federal League went belly up after the 1915 season, McGraw acquired Kauff, who appeared at the Giants' 1916 spring training camp in Texas with 52 bats and a pocketful of cash. He brashly announced that he would become the Ty Cobb of the National League.

McGraw liked Kauff and called him "a player of the old school. He thinks and lives baseball. That's the way I did when I was a youngster. . . . There aren't many players like that today."

But Kauff never lived up to his own billing. He stole 40 bases in 1916, but his batting average dropped to .264. Kauff remained with the Giants until 1920, when he was arrested and charged with auto theft. Although a jury acquitted him, Commissioner Landis, dissatisfied with the verdict, banned Kauff from baseball for life.

Royals manager Whitey Herzog (above, with catcher Darrell Porter and relief pitcher Al Hrabosky) led a bunch of gap hitters to AL West titles in 1976, 1977 and 1978. The Royals led the AL in doubles and triples in each of their division-winning seasons.

Yankees' Chris Chambliss in the bottom of the ninth inning of the final playoff game kept Herzog from the World Series.

Blending speed with power, the 1977 Royals won 102 games and coasted to a division championship. This time, the 5′ 5″ Patek, who was known as "the Flea," stole a league-leading 53 bases. Once again, a ninth-inning rally by the Yankees in the final playoff game kept the Royals from the World Series. The Yankees were spoilers a third time in 1978, when they dispatched Kansas City in the league championship series in four games. When the Royals finished second to California in 1979, in spite of a major league-leading 207 steals—83 by newcomer Willie Wilson—Herzog was fired.

But managers who win three division titles in four years do not remain out of work long. When the Cardinals struggled at the beginning of the 1980 season, Herzog was hired to replace Ken Boyer. He managed the club for 73 games until late August, and then took over as general manager on the condition that he could return to managing if he wanted to.

Turning the ballclub over to Red Schoendienst for the last month of the season, Herzog hit the road to evaluate the team's minor league talent. He concluded that the Cardinals had a number of veteran players who were producing minor league pennants, but that there were few major league prospects in the system. Back in St. Louis, he began to think about the kind of team he wanted to put together. The rule changes at the turn of the century had dictated the type of team John McGraw had fielded, but ballpark topography dictated the ballclub Herzog envisioned: "I drew up a master plan of what I wanted to do, the kind of team I wanted to build to accommodate the ballparks we played in," he said. Herzog noted that in the National

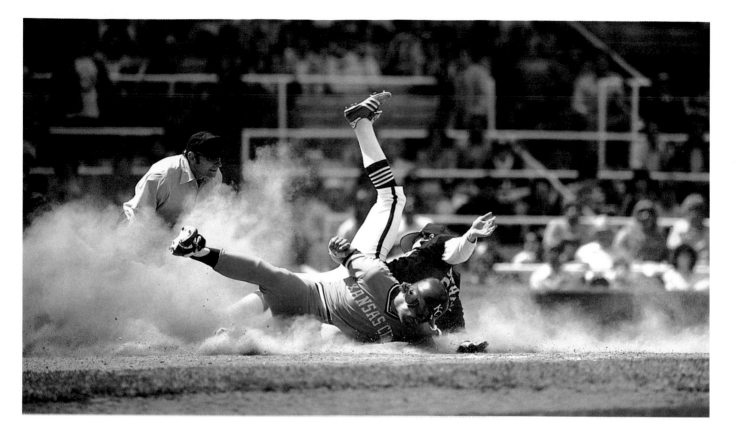

League, there were ten big ballparks where it was hard to hit home runs—six with artificial turf—and that Busch Stadium, with its deep fences and heavy summertime air, was the toughest hitter's park of all. He realized that speed, not power, was the key to winning at Busch: speed on the basepaths would help the Cardinals take advantage of balls hit on the turf, and speed in the outfield would help them to cut off hits before they could bounce off the turf to the wall. Herzog knew that the manager playing in Fenway Park or Wrigley Field could afford to wait for the three-run homer to win a game, but not at Busch: "In our place—and a lot of other places around the National League," he said, "you take your runs one at a time and hope for more. Hit the ball on the ground and run like hell. Steal a base, sacrifice, push the runner along, first-to-third them to death. I use the squeeze bunt as much as any manager in baseball, but in our park, it makes sense to give up an out for a run."

For manager Whitey Herzog, third baseman George Brett was a dream player. A brilliant hitter who was not afraid to get his uniform dirty, Brett hit an amazing .390 in 1980—the highest average for a third baseman since John McGraw hit .391 in 1899.

But Herzog was forced to admit that, except for shortstop Garry Templeton and outfielder Tony Scott, the 1980 Cards had very little speed. He needed better relief pitching to keep the team in close games, and he says, "I wanted to clean out the leadfoots and get us some guys who could run." Over the next two winters, general manager Herzog wheeled and dealed, while manager Herzog—he had reassumed that role—introduced inside baseball to St. Louis. Herzog, like McGraw, taught his team to chop down on the ball to get base hits. The Cards, however, needed no help from their grounds crew. On the artificial turf, the chopped ball naturally bounced high enough to make it almost impossible for an infielder to throw out a fast baserunner.

Stealing Pennants

Baseball's greatest dynasty — the New York Yankees — was built around power. But many of the game's other dynasties have been built around speed. Seven of John McGraw's ten pennant-winning Giant teams also led the NL in stolen bases. Whitey Herzog turned the trick three times in the 1980s with the Cardinals, while the Dodgers led the league in wins and steals eight times under three different managers from 1947 to 1965. Sparky Anderson's Reds won three NL pennants from 1972 to 1976, leading the NL in steals each time. Below is a look at these four dynasties in the years they won both the pennant and base-stealing title.

Pennant Winners	Year	W-L	PCT	SB	Leading base-stealer
New York Giants	1904	106-47	.693	283	Sam Mertes, 47
					Bill Dahlen, 47
	1905	105-48	.686	291	Art Devlin, **59**
	1911	99-54	.647	347	Josh Devore, 61
	1912	103-48	.682	319	Fred Snodgrass, 43
	1913	101-51	.664	296	George Burns, 40
	1917	98-56	.636	162	George Burns, 40
Brooklyn Dodgers	1947	94-60	.610	88	Jackie Robinson, **29**
	1949	97-57	.630	117	Jackie Robinson, **37**
	1952	96-57	.627	90	Pee Wee Reese, **30**
	1953	105-49	.682	90	Pee Wee Reese, 22
	1955	98-55	.641	79	Jim Gilliam, 15
Los Angeles Dodgers	1959	88-68	.564	84	Jim Gilliam, 23
	1963	99-63	.611	124	Maury Wills, **40**
	1965	97-65	.599	172	Maury Wills, **94**
Cincinnati Reds	1972	95-59	.617	140	Joe Morgan, 58
	1975	108-54	.667	168	Joe Morgan, 67
	1976	102-60	.630	210	Joe Morgan, 60
St. Louis Cardinals	1982	92-70	.568	200	Lonnie Smith, 68
	1985	101-61	.623	314	Vince Coleman, **110**
	1987	95-67	.586	248	Vince Coleman, **109**

Boldface indicates league leader.

Third baseman Terry Pendleton came up with the Cardinals in July 1984 and, according to Whitey Herzog, "changed our season around." Pendleton hit .324 and stole 20 bases in just 67 games. "Everyone seemed to take a cue from his aggressiveness."

In 1981 the Cards had the best overall record in the NL East, but because of the strike-shortened season and the playoffs between split-season leaders, they did not participate in postseason play. The 1982 Cards, featuring excellent runners like Lonnie Smith—with 68 steals and 120 runs—Willie McGee and Ozzie Smith, led the NL with 200 steals, 35 more than the second-best stealing club and 83 more than the Cards themselves had managed in 1980 before Whitey shuffled the deck. Practicing Herzog's motto, "run, boys, run," the Cards surprised the doubting Thomases and ran away with the 1982 world championship, despite hitting the fewest home runs of any team in baseball. Answering those skeptics after the season, Herzog said, "there were a lot of people around baseball . . . who couldn't believe the 1982 Cardinals were World Champions. . . . They seemed to think there was something wrong with the way we play baseball, with speed, and defense and line-drive hitters. They called it 'Whitey-ball' and said it couldn't last. Well, I don't know what 'Whitey-ball' is, unless it's the same kind of inside baseball that John McGraw was winning with eighty years ago."

Herzog is the first to admit that speed alone cannot win a pennant. In 1983 and 1984, despite leading the league in stolen bases, St. Louis was not a contender; the pitching and hitting just were not there. But by 1985, having acquired slugger Jack Clark from San Francisco and moving up speedster Vince Coleman from the farm system, the team had a potent offense to go along with a rejuvenated bullpen, with relievers like Jeff Lahti, Ken Dayley and Bill Campbell. The Cards scored a league-leading 747 runs and stole a remarkable 314 bases, 132 more than the runner-up Chicago Cubs. Coleman set a rookie record with 110 steals, McGee stole 56 bases

and Ozzie Smith, Andy Van Slyke and Tommy Herr each had more than 30. What's more, Coleman and McGee were on base so often that they contributed to a remarkable statistic for Herr, who hit behind them. Despite hitting only eight home runs on the season, Herr had 110 RBI, third in the league behind Atlanta's Dale Murphy and Cincinnati's Dave Parker, who hit 37 and 34 homers, respectively.

Even Herzog, the architect of all this running, was amazed when on August 1, 1985, the team stole four bases against the Cubs on a single pitch, Coleman and McGee executing a unique double double steal. Coleman was on second, McGee on first, when Herzog signaled a double steal. Cubs catcher Jody Davis threw to third base, where Coleman beat the tag but overslid the bag. Coleman started to scramble back to third, but finding the path blocked by third baseman Ron Cey, he headed for home. But Cey was chasing him toward an unguarded plate, and Coleman scored. In the confusion, McGee, already safe at second, took third. After several telephone calls and much debate, the official scorer determined the play should be ruled as four stolen bases.

Behind their running game, the Cardinals again made it to the World Series in 1985, where they faced the Kansas City Royals. Billed as a showdown for the bragging rights to Missouri, the Series was also a battle between two teams built in large part by the same proponent of inside baseball: Whitey Herzog. Both the Cards and the Royals could run and chase down fly balls in their large, artificial-surface ballparks.

But Coleman had been knocked down and out of postseason play before Game 4 of the NLCS by the automatic tarp that covers the turf at Busch Stadium. And his injury not only left a gap in the Cardinal lineup, it left a scar on

Giants catcher Bob Brenly tried a new way to slow down Cardinal speedster Andy Van Slyke, but in 1985 nobody could stop the Cardinals, who won 101 games largely with speed and great defense. "Nobody has ever had a faster or better defensive outfield than Coleman, McGee and Andy Van Slyke," said Whitey Herzog. Despite Brenly's tackle (above), Van Slyke scored.

Whitey Herzog has held just about every job baseball offers—player, coach, scout, field manager and general manager. "I've been thinking about baseball almost as long as I've been thinking," he said.

the team's morale. As Herzog said, "Coleman's injury took the flash out of our offense." The Cards, who had stolen six bases in the six-game league championship series against the Dodgers, could manage only two in seven games against the Royals, one less than K.C.'s Willie Wilson. Coleman's absence from the basepaths was particularly devastating to Herr. After batting .302 during the regular season and .333 in the NLCS, the second baseman hit a measly .154 in the Series. A bad call by umpire Don Denkinger in Game 6 didn't help the Cardinal cause, either. But they lost the Series in seven because, as Herzog said, "We just didn't play our brand of baseball."

Coleman was back on the basepaths in 1986 and in 1987, when he registered 109 of the Cards' major league-leading 248 steals. And St. Louis was back in the Series. It was Herzog's third appearance of the decade in the Series; no other manager in the 1980s could top that. But although Coleman stole another six bases in the World Series and the Cards stole 12 in all, St. Louis fell to the Cinderella Minnesota Twins in seven games. Sometimes speed is simply not enough. ⬡

Every time an AL pitcher turned around in 1980, there was Willie Wilson (opposite). The Royals left fielder had a major-league-record 705 at-bats, 230 hits, 79 stolen bases and 133 runs scored, while Whitey Herzog was in his first year as manager of the Cardinals. Five years later they were reunited in the World Series.

Don't
Look Back

hen baseball was still segregated, there was a clear difference between the styles of play in the Negro leagues and in the all-white major leagues. In a word, that difference was speed. The Negro leagues built their game around it, while the major leagues largely forgot about it after 1920. With the advent of the lively ball, power had become the password in both the American and National Leagues, and the home run trot dethroned the hit-and-run.

From the Roaring Twenties until the color barrier was broken in 1947, inside baseball was played mostly outside the major leagues. Like members of a shadow government waiting to resume power, talented black players and managers preserved and refined the bunt-run-steal-your-way-to-victory philosophy until the major leagues finally saw the light and integrated baseball. And just as blacks were at last integrated with whites on the ballfield, speed was integrated with power to revitalize the game.

The leader of this government-in-waiting, the man who had refined the aggressive approach, was Andrew "Rube" Foster, "the Father of Black Baseball." The son of a Texas preacher, Foster was a turn-of-the-century pitching star whose repertoire included a devastating screwball and a great pickoff move to second. According to pitching contemporary Bill Drake, Foster nailed many a runner at second by flipping the ball underhand to the base-

At 6' 4" and well over 200 pounds, Negro National League founder and manager Rube Foster (opposite) wasn't built for the running game; but all of his players were. "You couldn't hesitate with them on base," said pitcher Willie Powell. "If you hesitated, you were lost."

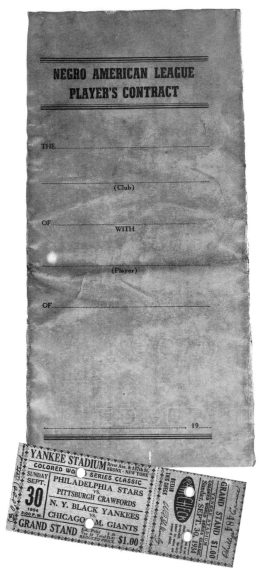

man behind him—without so much as turning around. In 1902, at 23, Foster
pitched for the Cuban Giants, a Chicago-based team composed of American
blacks. He is said to have won 51 games for the Giants that season—ten more
than any major leaguer has ever won.

In 1911 Foster teamed up with John Schorling, Charles Comiskey's
son-in-law, to form the Chicago American Giants, who went on to play at
the White Sox's old South Side Park. With Foster as manager, the Giants
became the top black team of the decade, practicing the kind of "scientific
baseball" that John McGraw's New York Giants were famous for. Dave
Malarcher, who played third base for Foster and later managed in the Negro
leagues, said of Foster, "Rube knew the value of speed, and he knew the
value of being able to fit into a directed play"—such as a bunt, hit-and-run or a
steal. "If [Ty] Cobb had had a smart manager like Rube Foster to make him fit
into the plays," Malarcher said, "[the Tigers] would have won pennant after
pennant after pennant."

Foster surely would have had the Tigers bunt—and bunt often. The
bunt was an integral part of his strategy, and other managers in the Negro
leagues began to pick up on it. Even as late as the 1930s, when white baseball
had become a home run contest, Webster MacDonald, manager of the
Philadelphia Stars, insisted that his players be ready and willing to sacrifice in
order to move teammates around the bases: "[If] you want to make an attack
on the other fellow, you got to keep a man in scoring position."

Foster always had a few players who could hit the long ball, but everyone in the lineup could bunt. Foster's practices included a drill in which players were instructed to bunt into a strategically placed hat. Said Malarcher,

"If they couldn't hit one pitcher, they would bunt him, be just as effective. That's what good baseball is. And that's what Rube Foster taught." So intent was Foster on playing the running game that he is said to have beaten a Negro league all-star with his meerschaum pipe for swinging away on a bunt sign.

One of Foster's many innovations was the hit-and-run bunt, and major league managers would come to watch his Giants execute it. When a fast runner reached first base, Foster would signal the batter to lay a bunt down the third-base line. The baserunner, taking off with the pitch, would have almost reached second by the time the hitter made contact. Instead of stopping, the runner continued to third base, which was unguarded because the third baseman was charging in to field the bunt. The ploy was difficult for opponents to counter: if the third baseman did not charge the ball, the batter would invariably reach first base, and the other runner would hold at second. Some speedsters, like Cool Papa Bell, scored from first base more than once on a hit-and-run bunt.

Foster also called for the play when the Giants managed to get an especially fast runner on second base. If the infielder tried to throw the batter out at first, the runner was instructed to charge past third and keep running.

Foster was not above resorting to other tricks. According to Cool Papa Bell, he built small ridges along the foul lines to guarantee that bunts by his players would stay fair. Former New York Lincoln Giants shortstop Frank "Strangler" Forbes said that Foster was "a mastermind" and "a thieving son of a bitch." Said Forbes: "He built his ball club with speed. We'd go out there to play those—excuse me—and you know what he does? We don't wise up until the end of the game, but he had drowned the goddam infield the night

The Chicago American Giants were molded in the image of manager Rube Foster, who taught his players every way imaginable to score runs. The Giants were a 1920s powerhouse in the Negro National League and, according to Hall of Famer Cool Papa Bell, "had the smartest players you ever saw."

5' 11" 190 lbs.   b 10/14/1896
BL TL   d 10/5/1954

OSCAR CHARLESTON
Outfield

Oscar Charleston was once clocked at 23 seconds in the 220-yard dash. His speed made him a great fielder, allowing him to play extremely shallow in center. It also earned him a nickname, "the black Ty Cobb." But Negro league expert John Holway argues that Charleston could run circles around Cobb in the outfield and hit for greater power, and that Cobb should have been called "the white Oscar Charleston."

Charleston, who played in the Negro leagues from 1915 until 1936, was aggressive—some said just plain mean —on the basepaths. Newt Allen, an infielder who played against Charleston, said: "The catcher would catch the devil when Charleston's scoring, because he would jump on you up at your chest, knock you down. Or one of the infielders, he'd run over him. He didn't care what you did to him, because he'd get his revenge some way."

While Charleston's viciousness on the bases was not universally applauded, his speedy outfield play was. Negro league star Cool Papa Bell argued that Charleston was a better fielder than Willie Mays and could chase down balls Mays would never have reached. Dave Malarcher, who played right field beside Charleston, said: "He could play all the outfield. I just caught foul balls. I stayed on the lines."

Charleston retired long before blacks were allowed to play in the major leagues but was elected to the Hall of Fame in 1976.

A five-time Negro National League All-Star, second baseman Sammy Hughes (above, right) played with the Elite Giants in Nashville, Columbus, Washington and Baltimore. Homestead Grays owner Cum Posey called him a "good hitter, crack fielder, and real baserunner."

before. Those suckers lay down a bunt, it rolls nine feet and stops. The man's on. My God, by the time you got to the ball the man was on." Forbes recalled that Foster was known to freeze baseballs to curb the power of teams who specialized in hitting the long ball: "You could feel them. If you held one long enough, your fingers stuck to the ball."

During the 1920s and 1930s, Foster's American Giants and other black teams derived a large part of their income from playing exhibition games against white semipro ballclubs and barnstorming "all-star" teams made up of major leaguers. After World War I, semipro baseball in Chicago began to lose its drawing power to the minor leagues and farm systems. So in 1920 Foster founded the first Negro league—the Negro National League—consisting of eight teams: the American Giants of Chicago, the Chicago Giants, the Detroit Stars, the St. Louis Stars, the Indianapolis ABCs, the Kansas City Monarchs, the Dayton Marcos and an itinerant team, the Cuban Stars. Foster also continued to manage the American Giants, a team that perfected the running game. The Giant lineup was lightning fast from top to bottom, and confident enough to bunt on third strikes, even in exhibition games against major leaguers. "When James Brown was catching we had seven men in the line-up could run a hundred yards in around ten seconds," Malarcher said. "All speed, and with Rube directing it, it was something. Rube telling us what to do—push it here, hit by the first baseman, hit over there. . . . When you play a diversified game, you don't allow your team to get into slumps, because you are making the breaks."

The team's first two batters were masters at the inside game. Leadoff hitter Jelly Gardner was a speedster who would bunt if the third baseman

played back, or chop it over his head if he played in. Bingo DeMoss was the ideal number-two hitter. If Gardner tried to steal second, DeMoss could wait until the last second before swinging. "He would save you, if he thought you were out," Gardner said. "He'd hit behind you."

As a bunter, DeMoss was a master at disguising his intentions. Instead of squaring around to bunt, he assumed a normal stance, making the opposition think he was hitting away and dropping the bat down at the last possible moment. And he had amazing control; more often than not, the ball bounced backward when it hit the turf. When Gardner was on base, he would be approaching second as DeMoss made contact, racing toward third, which was uncovered.

R ube Foster sometimes instructed the first man to reach base to take a long lead, just so his team could observe a pitcher's pickoff move. This gave the rest of the lineup an edge on the pitcher—an edge that they would take advantage of throughout the rest of the game. And Foster's teams had another unwritten rule intended to foil opposing hurlers: they were told not to swing at the first two pitches—a tactic designed to tire the pitcher by the seventh inning. Willie Powell, who played for Foster, said that Foster would pretend to signal plays with his pipe, and while opponents tried to decipher the pipe signals, the true sign was being sent by someone else.

Whoever was sending the signs, the result was that the aggressive Giants usually kept the opposition off balance. Foster himself once said: "The element of surprise in baseball is like everything else. We do what the other fellow does not expect us to do. . . . If you can run, if you're fast [your op-

Continued on page 104

Kansas City shortstop Jessie Williams (above, with Homestead Grays first baseman Buck Leonard in 1946) was best known for his glove, but came up big at the plate in big games. He went 4 for 8 in his two Negro National League All-Star appearances, and was the leading hitter in the 1942 World Series against the Homestead Grays with a .471 average.

Minnie Minoso

After a disappointing nine-game debut with Cleveland in 1949, Minnie Minoso came back big in 1951. In his first at-bat with Chicago, he smashed a 430-foot home run into the center field bullpen at Comiskey Park. Only two other players had ever done that. White Sox fans went wild and Minoso, one of the first black players in the majors, earned himself a place in the hearts of long-suffering White Sox fans.

Minoso's powerful bat, lightning speed and unbridled love for the game seemed to rejuvenate the Sox. During his rookie season, he hit .326 and led the league in triples with 14 and stolen bases with 31. He came in second—by just two votes—for Rookie of the Year. And by 1958 the second-division Sox began to finish in second or third place, earning the nickname the "Go Go Sox."

Minoso came to the big leagues after serving a long apprenticeship. Born in 1922, he grew up on a sugar cane plantation outside Havana and became one of the top players in Cuba while still a teenager. He signed with the New York Cubans and in 1947 led them to the Negro National League championship. After signing with the Cleveland Indians in 1948 and spending three seasons in the minors, he was traded to Chicago in 1951.

Although he was already 28 by the time he played his first full season in the majors, Minoso continued to improve. Sox owner Bill Veeck once said, "He's just like good bourbon. Gets better with age." Minoso went on to play in a total of 17 seasons, hitting over .300 eight times, leading the league in triples three times, in doubles once and in stolen bases three times. After he left the majors in 1964, he played in the Mexican League for another nine years. As a publicity stunt and a testament to his superb conditioning, he returned to the White Sox as a designated hitter in 1976, batted eight times that season and twice in 1980—when he was 57—becoming only the second major leaguer ever to play in five decades.

Minoso was a hit with AL fans. The left fielder was much loved for his enthusiasm and especially for his speed and daring on the basepaths. He regularly stretched singles into doubles and doubles into triples. He once joked, "I learn how to run fast in my native Cuba. I learn by stealing chickens!" Frank Lane, the Indians' general manager who brought the crowd-pleasing Minoso back to Cleveland in 1958, explained, "I felt Minnie was the one player in the American League who had that intangible quality of excitement that makes fans talk about him when they leave the park." Teammate Chico Carrasquel added, "He makes you want to play harder. Nobody sleeps with Minnie around."

The player some called "the Fountain of Youth" seemed to be impervious to injury. Once, in the first game of a doubleheader, he slid into first base so hard that he had to be carried from the field. Nevertheless, he begged to play in the second game. He did and won the game with a double. For the next three weeks, doctors drained blood and fluid from his leg regularly in the mornings, yet he was running on it by noon. He always crowded the plate and got hit with plenty of pitches. A Boston pitcher once beaned him and knocked him out. But Minoso amazed everyone by coming to, getting up, shaking his head a bit, stepping back into the batter's box and slapping out a game-winning triple. As Veeck noted, "I've never seen anyone who wanted to play as much as Minoso."

MINNIE MINOSO

Minnie Minoso was the kind of player who'd do anything to get on base, and as a result he led the AL in getting hit by pitched balls a record ten years, including six straight from 1956 to 1961. Minoso (below, stealing a base against Kansas City in 1960) also hit .300 in eight All-Star game appearances.

Outfield
Cleveland Indians 1949, 1951,
    1958–1959
Chicago White Sox 1951–1957,
    1960–1961, 1964, 1976, 1980
St. Louis Cardinals 1962
Washington Senators 1963

GAMES	**1,841**
AT-BATS	**6,579**
BATTING AVERAGE	
Career	**.298**
Season High	**.326**
SLUGGING AVERAGE	
Career	**.459**
Season High	**.535**
HITS	
Career	**1,963**
Season High	**184**
DOUBLES	
Career	**336**
Season High	**36**
TRIPLES	
Career	**83**
Season High	**18**
HOME RUNS	
Career	**186**
Season High	**24**
RUNS BATTED IN	
Career	**1,023**
Season High	**116**
RUNS	
Career	**1,136**
Season High	**119**
STOLEN BASES	
Career	**205**
Season High	**31**
STOLEN-BASE TITLES, AL	
	1951–1953

Third baseman Ray Dandridge (above, sliding) was in the twilight of his brilliant career by the time he got a shot with the Minneapolis Millers—the New York Giants' Class AAA farm team—in 1949. Dandridge hit .369 that season, and was the league's MVP in 1950. He never got called up to the majors, but was elected to the Hall of Fame in 1987.

ponent] has to make a perfect play, and if you surprise him, he can't make a perfect play."

Foster's Giants won pennants the first three years of the Negro National League's existence, and their style of play was soon widely adopted. J. G. Taylor Spink wrote in his *Sporting News:* "Recently, especially in games played in Chicago, the negro teams have shown wonderful speed and skill in their work. . . . They have developed the old high score game into regular aggressive low-scoring contests."

The style of play Spink extolled was on the rise in the Negro leagues, but it was waning in the majors. The Negro leaguers realized this, but they felt their running game was superior to the power game inspired by Babe Ruth and the other white sluggers. Pitching great Satchel Paige recalled how he had selected players for his barnstorming team: "I wasn't after no home run hitter. I only wanted a fellow who'd get a piece of the ball." Paige, who finally reached the majors in 1948 with the Cleveland Indians, posted a 6–1 record with a fine 2.48 ERA at the age of 42. And he claimed that his success was due to the fact that everyone tried to homer off him. "That was like cool water to me," he said.

Among the great Negro league base-stealers were Spottswood Poles and Willie Wells—both of whom proved themselves in contests against major league players. In 1911 Poles stole 41 bases in 60 Negro league games, and in the four games he played in against white major leaguers in which statistics were kept, he stole five. In 1929 Wells stole home with winning runs on two consecutive days against a major league all-star team. While neither Monte Irvin nor Roy Campanella ever stole home in a Negro league game, they both did it after they made the majors.

In the photo: EAST-WEST, MILTON K.C., GIBSON GRAYS., COOPER K.C.

In 1910 the Detroit Tigers journeyed to Havana to take on a Cuban team that included Negro league star John Henry Lloyd, called "the Black Honus Wagner." Everyone wondered how Ty Cobb, the greatest runner in the major leagues, would fare against the Cuban team. He didn't do so well; after stealing 65 bases during the regular season, Cobb was shut out on the basepaths in each of the five games he played. Lloyd himself tagged Cobb out three times in one game. Lloyd had a terrific series at the plate as well as in the field, batting .500. Cobb batted .369, but was so angry with the results that he vowed never to play against blacks again.

Despite the numbers, white ballplayers were convinced that few if any Negro leaguers were good enough for the big leagues. And although Negro league players often attended major league games, benefiting from what they observed, major leaguers rarely bothered to watch Negro league games. It wasn't until after World War II, when Jackie Robinson and other black players made it to the majors, that the Negro league's special brand of baseball crossed over.

ronically, only a year before he signed with the Brooklyn Dodgers, Robinson himself was uninitiated in the ways of Negro league ball. He had grown up in California and had played integrated sports until he joined the Kansas City Monarchs in 1945. As the season progressed, it became more and more apparent that Brooklyn Dodgers general manager Branch Rickey was going to select Robinson to break the color line. Recalling Rube Foster's dictum, "We have to be ready when the time comes for integration," some of the best players and coaches of the Negro leagues were determined to teach Robinson as much as they could in the few months they had. They knew that

Speed merchant Henry Milton played right field and batted leadoff for the Kansas City Monarchs during their glory years in the late 1930s. Milton was a five-time All-Star, and although he got tagged out by Josh Gibson of the Homestead Grays (above) in the 1939 All-Star Game, Milton and his West teammates rallied for three in the eighth in a 4–2 win.

*Josh Gibson's legend grew on the strength
of his titanic home runs, but in his prime
he was also one of the fastest players on
the Homestead Grays. Gibson hit .483
in nine Negro National League All-Star
Game appearances, including a double and
run scored in 1944 (right, sliding) at
Chicago's Comiskey Park.*

Robinson's failure in the major leagues could destroy hopes for integration for a long time to come.

But Robinson, a West Coast native and college graduate, was not receptive to advice from the countrified southerners and slick northeasterners who made up the Negro leagues. So the old-timers conspired to give him a crash course in the fine points of the game by showing him up on the field. Robinson was a shortstop at the time, and in one instance the aging Cool Papa Bell was brought in to teach Robinson that he wasn't as good as he thought he was at covering second base on steals. As Bell slid in under Robinson's tag for a stolen base, he said, "See that? They got a lot of guys in the major leagues slide like that. You can't get those guys out like that."

Whether it was tutoring or natural talent that made the difference, Robinson proved himself ready for integration, though many of his white opponents were caught off guard. In his first year as a Brooklyn Dodger, Robinson led the NL by stealing 29 bases and was voted Rookie of the Year.

By 1947 Rube Foster had been gone for two decades. He suffered a nervous breakdown in 1926 and died four years later at the age of 51. Still, the lessons he taught and the style of play he advocated survived and flourished, and eventually gave the game of baseball a new lease on life. ❶

*Jackie Robinson (opposite) broke major
league baseball's color line in 1947, and
attracted attention as much for his aggressive,
intimidating style of play as for his skin color.
"Like a few, very few athletes . . . Robinson
did not merely play at center stage,"
wrote Roger Kahn. "He was center stage;
and wherever he walked, center stage
moved with him."*

Jamu "Cool Papa" Bell

Cool Papa Bell

Long before Maury Wills, long before Lou Brock, long before Rickey Henderson, there was Cool Papa Bell. No one ran the bases better or faster. Because he spent his career in the Negro leagues, Bell never earned the fame of the others. But in some ways he deserved it more. He was the essence of speed in baseball, the man who epitomized the steady menace of fast legs. One year he allegedly stole as many as 175 bases in just under 200 games, although as with all of the early black stars, his achievements never made it into official record books. He always took the extra base, too, sometimes even on a bunt, streaking from first to third while the other team's players seemed dumbfounded.

Born James Thomas Bell in Starkville, Mississippi, in 1903, he was nicknamed "Cool Papa" while still in his teens. He was the most unflappable 17-year-old pitcher anyone on his first team in St. Louis had ever seen. Two years later, in 1922, he turned pro with the St. Louis Stars. He had a knuckleball that no one could hit. Unfortunately, almost no one could catch it, either. It also became very clear that Bell's speed was being wasted on the mound. He had already beaten Jimmy Lyons, then recognized as the fastest man in the league, in a race before one game. So in 1924, Bell became a full-time outfielder and went about creating a legend.

He was a thrilling center fielder, daring batters to try to hit the ball over his head and then running it down. He played so shallow that often he was used for pickoff plays at second base. Sometimes he even joined in rundowns on the bases, because if anyone could run an opponent down, he could. Bell, a natural right-hander, took advantage of his speed at the plate too, training himself to become a switch-hitter so he could more easily beat out drag bunts and high choppers. It became accepted wisdom around the league that if a grounder took more than two hops, Bell would beat it out. When he was at bat, infielders would move up, as if they were playing to cut off a runner at third. But Bell did not live by infield hits alone. He became a deft bat handler who could spray balls all over the field, and throughout his career, his batting average usually hovered in the high .300s.

More than anything else, though, Bell was a baserunner extraordinaire. He stood out in a league of speedsters, where runs were still created with explosive, savvy running, rather than the long home runs that had taken over in the majors. He haunted pitchers and catchers, once stealing second, third and home on consecutive pitches. Another time he stole two bases on one pitch—a pitchout, no less—when the catcher, stunned by Bell's speed, stood at the plate holding the ball. He made outfielders nervous too, routinely scoring from first on singles. In one game he hit three inside-the-park homers.

It didn't hurt Cool Papa's reputation when he beat the major league record by running the bases in just over 13 seconds on a muddy field. Bell claimed to have run it in 12 seconds on a dry field. And the tales grew taller. "Cool Papa hit a grounder through the box and was hit in the back with the ball as he slid into second," one story went. Another had it that "he

Bell (left, with the Chicago American Giants in 1942) was every bit as spectacular in the outfield as he was on the basepaths. Hall of Famer Paul Waner, who played in the era of Tris Speaker and Max Carey, called Bell "the smoothest center fielder I've seen."

Bell (below, sliding) was 40 when he joined the Homestead Grays in 1943, but helped the Grays win three straight Negro National League pennants, hitting .335 in the process.

Bell (ninth from left) starred for the Pittsburgh Crawfords in 1934, but was only one of four future Hall of Famers on the team. The others were first baseman Oscar Charleston (far right), pitcher Satchel Paige (second from right), and catcher Josh Gibson (third from right).

could turn out the light and be in bed before the room got dark." That one, attributed to Satchel Paige, actually had some basis in truth. As Bell told the story, he discovered one night that his hotel room had a slow, faulty light switch and so he was able to live up to his boast to Paige that he could be in bed before the light went out.

Even with his slender build—he was 5′ 11″ and weighed 140 pounds—Bell was a durable athlete, playing constantly for almost 29 seasons, plus 21 winters in Latin America. He played on three of the greatest clubs in the history of the Negro leagues: the St. Louis Stars from 1922 through 1931, the Pittsburgh Crawfords from 1933 through 1936 and the Homestead Grays from 1943 through 1946. He spent four of his prime years, from 1937 to 1940, in the Mexican leagues, where he earned his highest salary of $450 a month. Like most of his peers, Bell was too old to play in the majors by the time the color line fell, but he did his part to make sure younger black players got their best shot at making it big.

When it became clear that Jackie Robinson would probably be the first to make the move, some of the veteran black players were nervous. They knew Robinson was inexperienced and were worried that he might fail. It would help if they could convince him that shortstop wasn't his best position, and Bell was recruited to help make that point. Before one game the road secretary of Robinson's team, the Kansas City Monarchs, asked Bell to hit the ball into the hole at short, where Robinson was not a strong fielder. Twice Bell obliged, and though he was in his forties, he beat Robinson's throw both times. He also stole four bases that night, several times stepping around Robinson's tag. Robinson got the message: in the majors, he played first and second. In 1946 Bell also gave a boost to Monte Irvin's chances to switch leagues. Bell, hitting over .400, was leading Irvin for the Negro National League batting title, but sat out the last game of the year so he wouldn't have enough games to qualify for it. Irvin became batting champion and three years later moved to the New York Giants.

Bell started his long pro career with the St. Louis Stars (left), but most baseball fans never got a chance to see him play. By the time Jackie Robinson broke the color barrier in 1947, Bell was 43 years old. "They say that I was born too soon," he said. "I say the doors were opened up too late." In 1974 (below) he became the fifth Negro league player elected to the Hall of Fame.

There's little question that Bell would have starred in the majors if he'd had a chance. In exhibition games against major league players, he hit .391. And he enjoyed his last moment of glory in 1948 against a big-league all-star team featuring Bob Lemon. Bell didn't want to play in the game; he said he was too out of shape. But pitching star Satchel Paige persuaded Bell to play. Batting against Lemon, Bell singled and was followed by Paige, who bunted the ball toward third. Bell easily made it to second, but he didn't stop there when he saw the third baseman was out of position. Then, when the catcher ran out to try to cover the bag, Bell blew right by him and made it home before Lemon could cover the plate. Cool Papa had scored from first on a bunt. He was 45 years old.

It was 26 more years before Cool Papa Bell finally got his due. In 1974 he was inducted into the Hall of Fame with Mickey Mantle, Whitey Ford and umpire Jocko Conlin. It was fitting recognition for the man Bill Veeck called "the most magical player I have ever seen."

Laying
It Down

"An' another thing I asks him. I used to be the greatest sacrifice hitter in baseball. So I asks him. 'Young man, can you bunt?' 'Mister Ryan,' says he . . . 'I don't like to brag about myself, but I can bunt farther than any other man on the team!' Them's his very words. Can you beat it?"

—from a 1917 baseball story in McClure's Magazine *by Jerome Beatty*

Bill Bailey's bunting style (above) didn't impress the 1911 Yankees, who cut the outfielder after just five games. Bailey's major league career consisted of nine at-bats and one hit.

Nobody expects pitchers to be able to hit, but in the NL they can help themselves out with a timely bunt or two. In 1977 St. Louis rookie John Urrea (38, preceding page) laid one down in front of charging Giants first baseman Willie McCovey and under the watchful eye of on-deck hitter Lou Brock. Urrea hit .138 that season.

s the 1951 baseball season raced toward its conclusion, the New York Yankees and the Cleveland Indians were engaged in another heated battle for the American League pennant. In September the Indians went to New York for a series that would in all likelihood determine the league championship. The score was tied, 1–1, in the bottom of the ninth with the bases loaded and one out when Phil Rizzuto, the smallest Yankee at 5' 6" and 150 pounds, was about to face the Tribe's Bob Lemon. But before he stepped up to the plate, the Yankees' third-base coach, Frank Crosetti, called Rizzuto over and told him to try the suicide-squeeze bunt. For Rizzuto, the best bunter on the team, the challenge was clear: make contact with the ball, or Joe DiMaggio, who was on third and would be taking off with the pitch, would be a dead duck and the Yanks' rally would be snuffed out.

"The first pitch was low and the umpire called it a strike," Rizzuto recalled. "I deliberately made a big squawk on the call. The trick must have worked, because none of the infielders were moving up. The pitch was a good one to bunt, but they sometimes pitch out on that first one and nail the runner coming home. We had decided to play it safe and signal the squeeze for the second pitch. DiMaggio made the play work. He didn't start too soon. Lemon had no idea Joe was coming until it was too late. Suddenly, with the pitch on its way and Joe breaking for home, I dumped the ball down and that was the ball game. . . . It was a big one to win."

The bunt is the ultimate weapon of the player—or team—who has speed, but not power. "I know I can't depend on slugging power to move men around the bases, so the bunt does much of the work for me," Rizzuto wrote in 1952. "Take a look at the good bunters in the big leagues—Johnny Pesky,

While the rest of the Yankees were swinging for the fences in the early 1950s, shortstop Phil Rizzuto was winning games by holding his bat in one place. Each year that Rizzuto led the AL in sacrifice bunts—1949 to 1953—the Yankees won a world title. "Bunting is one of the few arts in baseball that can be taught," he said. "You can't teach power or speed."

Checking his swing was not a familiar activity for Yankee outfielder Omar Moreno, even when bunting. Playing for the Pittsburgh Pirates, Moreno led the NL in steals in 1978 and 1979, but struck out 104 times each season.

Dom DiMaggio, Bobby Avila, Nelson Fox, Pee Wee Reese and Richie Ashburn are among the best. Like me, they are relatively small and fast. They can move the runner over pretty consistently with the bunt. Sure, we all hit the occasional homer, but the bunt is one of our bread-and-butter talents."

The bunt was made popular, appropriately enough, by one of the smallest men ever to play the game: Dickey Pearce of the original Brooklyn Atlantics. Pearce stood only 5' 3" tall, or as the *New York Journal's* Sam Crane wrote, "The little fellow was not bigger than a good sized cruller." Nevertheless, Crane pointed out, Pearce was the most feared player in the 1866 Brooklyn lineup. "[His] short, pudgy legs brought in more tallies . . . than all the slugging sprinters there were on the team. And why? Simply because Dickey Pearce knew how to get to first base."

One of the ways Pearce got to first base was with the tactic he perfected called the fair-foul hit. The idea was to chop down on the ball to make it hit in fair territory first and then bound off foul between the catcher and third base. Such a ball would be ruled foul today, but not when Pearce played; then, infielders were forced to chase after balls that had bounded well outside the baselines. Pearce and other speedsters often made it to second base on the play, and occasionally even reached third. Though Pearce didn't think that his fair-foul hit was anything special, it is a clear forerunner of the bunt. "It was not known as a bunt at that time and Dickey himself had no idea that he was making baseball history," wrote Crane.

It wasn't until 1876 that the play was popularized by Tim Murnane of the Boston Red Stockings of the National League. Murnane hit the ball with a customized flat-sided bat, a tactic that was initially called "butting." Pearce

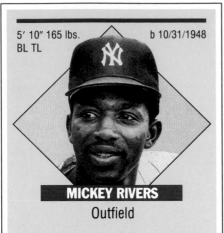

5' 10" 165 lbs.   b 10/31/1948
BL TL

MICKEY RIVERS
Outfield

Dubbed "Mick the Quick," John Milton "Mickey" Rivers was one of the fastest men in baseball in the mid-1970s. He turned in a stellar performance for the California Angels in 1975, leading the American League in triples with 13 and stolen bases with 70.

In December 1975 Rivers was traded to New York, where he contributed his remarkable speed to a Yankee team already blessed with solid pitching and powerful hitting. In his first year with New York, Rivers hit .312, scored 95 runs and stole 43 bases. He was the leadoff hitter and spark plug that helped the Yanks win the pennant that year —and the next year and the year after that.

Rivers spoke his own language. Of his Yankee experience, Rivers said he, Billy Martin and George Steinbrenner were "two of a kind." And he once claimed, "I want to hit .300, score 100 runs and stay injury prone."

Rivers meant well; teammate Oscar Gamble said, "He's got one of the nicest hearts you'd ever want to see." But Rivers liked to play the horses, liked to ask the Yankees for salary advances and liked to show up for games on his own time schedule. In 1979 Rivers was traded to the Texas Rangers.

In his last three years with the Rangers, Rivers was a designated hitter, wrapping up his career in 1984 by posting a .300 average in 313 at-bats. His professional career wasn't over, however; later he appeared as a professional bingo player under the name Miguel Rivera.

Shortstop Larry Bowa parlayed great speed, fine defense and bunting ability into a sparkling 16-year career. Bowa played in five All-Star games, five NL Championship Series and hit .375 with three steals in the Phillies' 1980 World Series win.

and Murnane used the tactic—whatever one calls it—to reach base. But by the turn of the century, batters were also "sacrificing" themselves—giving up an out by bunting to move a baserunner into scoring position.

Bunting—whether used to get the batter on base or to move up a runner—was particularly popular during the dead-ball era, when runs were dear and speed was essential. Ty Cobb was a master of the art. Pitching great Walter Johnson confessed that "the Georgia Peach" frustrated him time and again with his bunts for base hits. And even stars like Cobb were often called upon to execute the sacrifice bunt.

In the era of scientific baseball, failure to execute could be fatal. Alibi Ike, Ring Lardner's fictional ballplayer who captivated America in 1914, found that out his rookie year. In Lardner's short story, "Alibi Ike," the hero misses a bunt sign and hits a home run. In those days, a round tripper was something of a rarity, but Ike's manager, Cap, is not impressed. When Ike comes back to the dugout, Cap confronts him:

"When I say bunt, I mean bunt," says Cap.

"You didn't say bunt," says Ike, who, true to his name, has an excuse for everything.

"I says lay it down," says Cap. "If that didn't mean bunt, what does it mean?"

"Lay it down means bunt all right," says Ike, "but I understood you to say 'lay on it.' "

"All right," says Cap, "and that little misunderstanding will cost you $50."

Had he played a few years later, Ike wouldn't have had to worry. As the ball became livelier and it took more runs to win, heroes were determined by

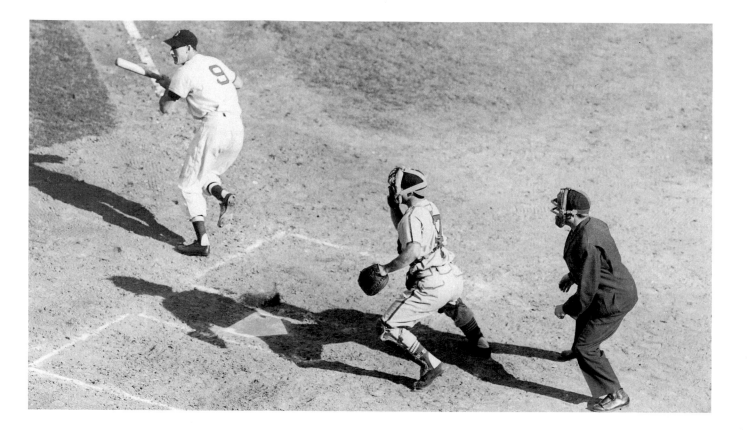

the number of home runs they hit, and the bunt itself became a rarity. As late as 1969, *Boston Globe* columnist Ray Fitzgerald lamented that bunting had become a lost art: "See the skinny little baseball player. See him dig in at the plate. Watch him swing his puny 31-ounce bat from the end trying to hit home runs. See him strike out. That's the way it has been for a long time. The homer is king and the man who knows how to bunt is lost in the crowd."

Fitzgerald recalled spring training of 1967, when the Red Sox' less-than-speedy Carl Yastrzemski told reporters that he was going to bunt at least once during every exhibition game to "keep the infielders honest." But Yaz wasn't being honest himself. In the first game, he bunted a line drive to the opposing first baseman. That turned out to be his last bunt of the year.

Yastrzemski won the Triple Crown that season without bunting. Some saw that as evidence that bunting, or at least sacrifice bunting, is simply not an efficient way to generate runs. But if it hadn't been for a bunt, the Red Sox might not have won the pennant that year. In their final game of the season, Yaz and company faced the Minnesota Twins; the Sox needed the win to give them a chance at the league championship. And thanks to a seventh-inning rally ignited by pitcher Jim Lonborg's bunt single, Boston did win, and runner-up Detroit handed the Sox the pennant by losing a game to California.

Baltimore Orioles manager Earl Weaver was one of those who wasn't convinced that the bunt has value as an offensive tool: "I've got nothing against the bunt—in its place," he said. "But most of the time that place is in the bottom of a long-forgotten closet." Noting that a team's most precious possessions on offense are its 27 outs, Weaver believes that the risk involved in bunting—especially sacrifice bunting—is too

Continued on page 120

Frustrated by his 1 for 7 performance in the first two games of the 1946 World Series against St. Louis, Boston's Ted Williams resorted to bunting for a hit against the defensive shift that placed three infielders to the right of second base. Williams' bunt went for a hit, but he didn't try the tactic again in the Series, and wound up hitting just .200 as the Cardinals beat Boston in seven games.

BERT CAMPANERIS
ONE OF BASEBALL'S GREATEST MOMENTS

Hits 2 Homers in First Major League Game.

Bert Campaneris

Had the Kansas City A's coaching staff been more democratic, Bert Campaneris might never have made it to the major leagues. And the A's, after they moved to Oakland in 1968, might never have won three straight world titles.

Campaneris was signed as a catcher in 1962, but when the A's coaches got a look at the 140-pound youngster from a tiny village in Cuba, they were unimpressed. All except Robbie Robertson, manager of the A's Class A team in the Florida State League. "All others on the staff wanted to give him his release," said scouting director Ray Swallow. "But Robbie wanted to make a utility man out of Campy. Fortunately we have a rule. If one member of our staff wants to keep a man, he stays—even if all others vote against keeping him."

Utility didn't quite cover what Campaneris did for Robertson in 1962. He played catcher, first base, shortstop and center field, and even turned in three relief appearances on the mound. In one two-inning stint, he allowed one run and one hit while striking out four, which wasn't so unusual, except that the ambidextrous Campaneris pitched right-handed to the right-handed batters and left-handed to the left-handed batters.

Campaneris finally settled in at shortstop, and his hitting and base-stealing ability earned him a quick trip to the majors. He was hitting .325 for Class AA Binghamton when he was called up midway through the 1964 season. He made an immediate, indelible impression. The first pitch Campaneris saw was from Minnesota's Jim Kaat, and he parked it. In the seventh inning, he did it again to become the third player ever to homer twice in his first major league game.

In 1965, his first full season, Campaneris led the AL with 51 stolen bases and started a string of five straight seasons with at least 50 steals. No one to that date—not Cobb, not Wills, not Brock—had stolen at least 50 in each of his first five seasons. Campaneris also found himself the center of one of owner Charlie Finley's promotional stunts on September 8, when he played all nine positions in a game.

Finley's A's matured into a dynasty in the 1970s and, despite his erratic fielding, Campaneris was a central figure in the team's success. His raw speed and quick start earned him six base-stealing titles and an average of 46 steals a season from 1965 through 1976. And he was unusually strong for his size, as he showed in 1970 when he hit 22 home runs, almost four times his previous high.

Campaneris played on five straight AL West champions and on three straight world champions. His brightest postseason came in 1973, when he hit .333 with two home runs and three stolen bases in the A's ALCS win over Baltimore, then had nine hits, scored six runs and made three steals as the A's beat the Mets in the World Series. Campy won Game 3 with a single in the 11th, then broke open a scoreless Game 7 with a two-run homer in the third. His dimmest postseason experience came in 1972, when, after being hit on the ankle by a pitch, he was suspended from the ALCS for throwing his bat at 6' 5", 220-pound Tiger pitcher Lerrin LaGrow. The incident showed that while Campaneris was quiet and shy off the field, on the field he was anything but. Like all great base-stealers, he was aggressive, almost to the point of cockiness. "I'll tell you about him," said Mel McGaha, who managed Campaneris in 1964. "One day he made three errors and the fans were getting on him. After the third error he tipped his hat to the crowd. It takes a little guts for a rookie to react that way."

BERT
CAMPANERIS

Shortstop
Kansas City Athletics 1964–1967
Oakland Athletics 1968–1976
Texas Rangers 1977–1979
California Angels 1979–1981
New York Yankees 1983

GAMES	2,328
AT-BATS	8,684
BATTING AVERAGE	
Career	.259
Season High	.290
SLUGGING AVERAGE	
Career	.342
Season High	.448
HITS	
Career	2,249
Season High	177
DOUBLES	
Career	313
Season High	29
TRIPLES	
Career	86
Season High	12
HOME RUNS	
Career	79
Season High	22
RUNS BATTED IN	
Career	646
Season High	64
RUNS	
Career	1,181
Season High	97
STOLEN BASES	
Career *(9th all time)*	649
Season High	62
STOLEN-BASE TITLES, AL	
1965–1968, 1970, 1972	
WORLD SERIES	**1972–1974**

Bert Campaneris was never a great hitter, and his play at shortstop left a lot to be desired. But his speed, guile and aggressiveness made him a key to the Oakland dynasty of the 1970s. "He has all kinds of guts," said Jackie Robinson.

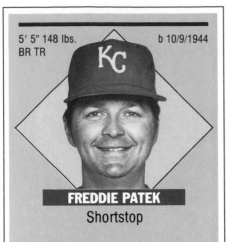

5′ 5″ 148 lbs.
BR TR

b 10/9/1944

FREDDIE PATEK
Shortstop

At 5′ 5″, Freddie Patek was considered too small to play ball—even high school baseball. In his senior year he finally got a chance to play and wound up leading the team in batting average and stolen bases. He made it to the minors with Gastonia of the Western Carolina League in 1966, and in his first 75 games he hit .310 and stole 38 bases, but he still got that disbelieving look each time a coach sized him up.

In 1968 Patek joined the Pittsburgh Pirates. He was the smallest man in the majors. And even though Patek played 147 games in 1969, Pirate coaches thought he was too fragile for full-time duty. So after the 1970 season, Patek was traded to Kansas City. The Royals' manager, Hall of Fame pitcher Bob Lemon, respected Patek's determination and said, "Fred plays every game like it's the seventh game of the World Series."

Lemon's faith paid off. In 1971 Patek hit .267, stole 49 bases and led the league in triples. But the intensity that earned Patek his place in the majors also put him in the hospital on the verge of nervous exhaustion in 1972. Patek recovered quickly enough to continue his streak—more than 30 stolen bases in eight straight seasons, from 1971 through 1978.

Along the way, Patek learned to lighten up. Asked how it felt to be the smallest player in the major leagues, he quipped, "It's better than being the smallest player in the minor leagues."

When you can hit like Cubs outfielder Dwight Smith—.324 as a rookie in 1989 —managers don't ask you to sacrifice too often. Smith had just three sacrifice bunts in 1989, but his speed makes him a constant threat to bunt for a hit.

great. The team that elects to bunt is depending on a series of not-so-dependable events: that the batter will get his bat on the ball for the bunt; that he will place it well; that the bunt will advance the baserunner; and that, with one less out in the inning, the team will be able to get the runner home. Even if the team does manage to score that one run off the sacrifice, Weaver argues, it has turned down the opportunity to go for the big inning. "If you play for one run, that's all you'll get," says Weaver, who was famous for playing for the three-run homer and the big inning.

With the designated hitter taking the place of the pitcher in the batting order, most AL managers feel that it doesn't make much sense to play for one run. The DH is one of several factors that has led to the absence of the bunt in recent years. Artificial turf has also cut down on the number of bunts; since the ball is more lively on the turf, only those hitters with tremendous bat control can bunt successfully. Economics and ego have had an effect, too; big hitters are paid for big hits, not bunts. In a game against Kansas City in July 1977, Yankees manager Billy Martin flashed the bunt sign to slugger Reggie Jackson, starting a now-famous incident. After the first pitch, Martin took the bunt sign off, but Jackson was already so angry that he had been asked to bunt that he continued to bunt and foul off pitches until he struck out, losing the game for New York.

Still, when executed by a speedster with good bat control, a bunt can make some infielders desperate. In a May 1981 game between Seattle and Kansas City, Royals center fielder Amos Otis laid a dribbler down the third-base line and took off for first. Mariner third baseman Lenny Randle approached the ball on his hands and knees. Eventually, the ball rolled foul.

K.C. manager Jim Frey ran out onto the field, insisting that Randle had been blowing on the ball to make it roll foul, and the umpire agreed, crediting Otis with a hit. After the game Randle defended himself: he hadn't been blowing on the ball, he said, he had been pleading with it.

San Francisco's Robby Thompson would be the perfect number-two hitter—if he didn't strike out so much. In 1986 Thompson set a team record with 18 sacrifice bunts but also struck out 112 times.

The term "sacrifice"—bunting to move the runner up—has affected the way the strategy developed. "The whole thing was a misunderstanding!" says baseball historian Bill James. "They called it a 'sacrifice,' and the players got so caught up with the nobility of the idea that they figured you were actually supposed to surrender yourself at first base." Henry Chadwick, the Father of Baseball, voiced the same concern in 1895: "A majority of batsmen seem to be of the impression that . . . all they have to do is go to bat and have themselves put out, so that the baserunner at first base may be able to reach second base. This is a very erroneous idea of the true intent of a sacrifice hit," Chadwick wrote. "No skillful batsman ever goes to the bat purposely to hit the ball to have himself put out; that would be a very silly move. On the contrary, he takes his bat in his hand every time with the primary object of making a base hit if he possibly can."

Chadwick, Weaver and friends notwithstanding, the pure sacrifice has had its proponents in recent years. In 1982, when American League teams averaged only 54 sacrifice bunts for the season and National League teams averaged 82, the California Angels were successful on 114 attempts; Tim Foli alone sacrificed 26 times. The Angels, managed by Gene Mauch, who loved to bunt, won their division that year.

Yet the bunter need not be a sacrificial lamb. Speedsters like the Cardinals' Vince Coleman and the Cubs' Jerome Walton, and savvy bat handlers

It's not just how many times a player steals that counts, but also how often he gets away with it. In 1922, Max Carey stole 51 bases — nowhere near Rickey Henderson's record 130 — but Carey was caught just twice. Below are the players who stole at least 50 bases and turned in the top 15 single-season success rates. Tim Raines dominates the list with high-percentage performances four years in a row, 1984 through 1987.

Player	Year	SB	CS	SB%
1. Max Carey	1922	51	2	.962
2. Jerry Mumphrey	1980	52	5	.912
3. Tim Raines	1987	50	5	.909
4. Eric Davis	1987	50	6	.893
5. Maury Wills	1962	104	13	.889
Rickey Henderson	1985	80	10	.889
7. Willie Wilson	1980	79	10	.888
8. Tim Raines	1985	70	9	.886
Tim Raines	1986	70	9	.886
10. Bert Campaneris	1969	62	8	.886
11. Vince Coleman	1986	107	14	.884
12. Tim Raines	1984	75	10	.882
13. Willie Wilson	1983	59	8	.881
14. Eric Davis	1986	80	11	.879
15. Rickey Henderson	1988	93	13	.877

like the White Sox' Ozzie Guillen have increased their batting averages by regularly bunting for hits. Seven-time batting champion Rod Carew took daily bunting practice while he was in the majors, claiming that bunting for the hit added 25 points to his batting average.

With more than 130 bunts for hits in his career, the Giants' fleet center fielder Brett Butler may be the game's top bunter. When he broke into the majors, Butler had difficulty hitting. After the 1983 season, Braves hitting coach Bob Watson suggested Butler work on his bunting. "Bob basically told me to make the best use of the gifts God gave me and not try for ones I didn't have," Butler says. "I could always run, and bunting just emphasized that." Butler taught himself to use a hitting stride that disguised his intention as he slid his hands into bunting position. The results were dramatic. Butler increased his number of bunt singles from three in 1983 to 29 in 1984.

The debate over the wisdom of bunting continues, but the bunt remains a potential weapon in most teams' arsenals. The first thing a hitter does when he enters the cage for batting practice is to lay down a bunt. But how often it seems that broadcasters—and fans, too—wonder aloud why the speedster in the lineup doesn't try to bunt for base hits, or why the team's slugger doesn't lay one down and surprise the infield playing deep on the edge of the outfield. Still, those in the Earl Weaver school of managing currently outnumber the disciples of Gene Mauch.

But as long as there are heady players willing to sacrifice ego for the sake of the team, the tradition started by Pearce will always be a part of the game. Says Brett Butler: "I don't think bunting will ever die. It will come back because there will always be some little guy somewhere who won't take no for an answer and who will be determined to take his gifts to the limits."

When Giants outfielder and leadoff hitter Brett Butler (opposite) laid down a bunt in 1988, more often than not he beat it out. Butler had 20 bunt hits—a league high—in just 37 tries that season, a .541 clip. He also led the NL with 109 runs scored.

Rod Carew

A part-time scout for the Minnesota Twins plucked Rod Carew off a New York City sandlot diamond in 1964. Off the field, the 19-year-old was quiet and drew little notice. But on the field his bat said plenty; his smooth stroke and superb bat control—evident even in the confines of a city playground—earned him a tryout with the Twins when they came to New York for a series against the Yankees.

Carew's bat continued to make noise once he was signed. He came up from the minors to play second base for the Twins in 1967 and batted .292—56 points above the league average and good enough to earn him Rookie of the Year honors.

Carew is a national hero in his native Panama, even though he has spent most of his adult life in the United States. He retains his Panamanian citizenship, he says, because it "gives the children there someone to look up to. They need that." He should know. As a boy, Carew played baseball both as an escape from day-to-day misery and as a ticket out of poverty. He recalled many days when sugar water was his only meal and many when he had no meal at all. His family life, too, was less than idyllic: "I remember we went hungry while [my father] brought food home and kept it in his room, daring us to touch it. One day my brother ate some chicken [my father] had hidden, and I thought [my father] was going to kill him over it." Luckily, Carew could play baseball: "It saved me. I loved it, played all the time, and I could hit from the time I picked up a bat."

In 1969, his third year in the majors, Carew won his first of seven batting titles; only Ty Cobb and Honus Wagner won more, and only Stan Musial and Rogers Hornsby won as many. In 1977, his best year, he hit .388 and won the AL's MVP Award. In 1972 Carew did something no other batting champion ever did: he won an AL batting title without hitting a single home run, a telling statistic. The key to his success as a hitter was bat control—sacrificing power for finesse. Over his 19-year career, Carew averaged fewer than five home runs a season, and nearly four out of five of his career hits were singles. "Home runs don't particularly interest me," he said, "but hits do." And slapping out less spectacular hits gave Carew a more-than-spectacular consistency. As Angels teammate Doug DeCinces said, "The difference between this guy and the rest of us is that when we get hot, we go up to .300. When he gets hot, he goes up to .500."

Despite his numbers at the plate, Carew was accused of being lazy. But that was an illusion; his batting style was so fluid and so smooth that he appeared not to try. As Angels shortstop Tim Foli said, "He does things people take for granted because he's so smooth." Second baseman Bobby Grich felt the same way: "He makes hitting look so effortless. You watch him and you say to yourself, 'Boy, that looks easy.' Then you get up there and pop one up." But Carew insisted that hard work, not natural talent, accounted for his phenomenal success. "I take a lot of extra batting practice," he said. "I've worked a lot more and a lot harder than a lot of guys."

Opposing pitchers could vouch for Carew's intensity—which was often hidden beneath his quiet exterior. He had great concentration, as do most

Rod Carew was pretty happy as a Minnesota Twin (left) until September 1978, when owner Calvin Griffith publicly called him "a damn fool" for having signed a 1976 contract for $170,000 a year. Carew demanded a trade, and wound up as an Angel (below) for $900,000 a year.

great hitters, but he also had a relentless drive to win, as Red Sox pitcher Dennis Eckersley found out. "One day [in 1978] I was absolutely red hot," Eckersley recalls, "leading 8–0 in the ninth inning up at Fenway. I happened to come in too tight on Rod . . . and he glared at me, squirting tobacco juice on the plate, muttering just loud enough for me to hear. Now why should I *ever* throw at Rod Carew? It's insane. Well, he bunted with two strikes for a hit and stole second on the first pitch. Why would anyone steal second, eight runs down with two outs in the ninth? As I was leaning in to get the sign, I heard some very cruel comments from second base. Then I realized Carew had stolen second to get a little closer to me, so that when I turned around he could talk to me without the crowd noise interfering. . . . Off the field he's a great person, but between the lines, a total gamer."

Carew thrived on the tension between pitcher and batter, and seemed to delight in making pitchers' lives miserable. "The most enjoyable feeling," he once said, "is to be in the on-deck circle and look at that s.o.b. and see him looking at you instead of the hitter and have him think, 'Jeez, how am I going to get this s.o.b. out?' "

Still, Carew *did* look awfully comfortable at the plate—not like someone who was about to face a barrage of 90-plus-mph pitches. But relaxing, as Carew explained it, was part of the science of hitting. "I relax the upper part of my body. I don't squeeze the bat. If you do, you lose flexibility. When the pitch comes I can direct my bat many ways." He even developed a special batting stance for when he was injured. "I cut down on the swing, use my hands more, take a shorter stride."

Carew was willing to challenge pitchers on the basepaths, too. He averaged 19 stolen bases a season, and on May 18, 1969, in a game against Detroit, he became a member of the elite group of players who have performed triple steals. His most impressive base-stealing performance also occurred in 1969, when he tied the major league record by stealing home seven times in eight attempts. The man who persuaded him to steal home in the first place was one of baseball's gamest managers, Billy Martin. And Martin insisted that Carew made it safely eight times but was robbed of a perfect record by a bad call. "The umpire was down on the play," Martin said. "He made the call lying on his back. He couldn't see it. Carew was safe."

Stealing home successfully so many times made an impression on AL pitchers. Nearly a decade after setting his record, Carew was still feared. Of his 1978 performance he said, "I stole home only once last year, but scored four times on walks. This has to tell you that some pitchers, especially young ones, are worried."

Despite his impressive hitting and baserunning, Carew was one of the most underpaid stars in baseball—partly because he was quiet, partly because he didn't hit the long ball. After 12 years with Minnesota, and a feud over his salary with Twins owner Calvin Griffith, he was traded to the California Angels.

Carew has always treasured his solitude, and by 1983 he had grown weary of being in baseball's spotlight for nearly two decades: "I get tired of it all," he said. "I could be happy away from it." Perhaps it was his .339 average that season that kept him playing. Two years later, the 39-year-old Carew hit .280, marking the end of his baseball career. It would've been a solid season for an average player. But Carew, whose .328 career mark placed him ahead of immortals like Jimmie Foxx, Roberto Clemente and Joe DiMaggio, was never average.

Carew's bat control (opposite) was legendary, but his baserunning also drew raves. "There are a number of guys who know how to steal as well as Rod," said Twins manager Frank Quilici. "But there's nobody alive who can turn a single into a double, or a double into a triple the way Rod can."

ROD
CAREW

First Base, Second Base
Minnesota Twins 1967–1978
California Angels 1979–1985

GAMES	2,469
AT-BATS	9,315
BATTING AVERAGE	
Career	.328
Season High	.388
SLUGGING AVERAGE	
Career	.429
Season High	.570
HITS	
Career	3,053
Season High	239
DOUBLES	
Career	445
Season High	38
TRIPLES	
Career	112
Season High	16
HOME RUNS	
Career	92
Season High	14
RUNS BATTED IN	
Career	1,015
Season High	100
RUNS	
Career	1,424
Season High	128
STOLEN BASES	
Career	353
Season High	49
ROOKIE OF THE YEAR	1967
MOST VALUABLE PLAYER	1977

Center Stage

Before the beginning of the 1954 season, New York Giants manager Leo Durocher told center fielder Willie Mays to cover everything he could in right field as well as center. Mays followed orders—pleasing Durocher but angering the team's right fielder, the slow-footed Don Mueller. Mueller's anger was aroused even further on the final day of the season, when Mays overtook him to win the National League batting title, .345 to .342.

The day after the season ended, the Giants, who had won the pennant, gathered at the Polo Grounds for a team picture. As Mays stood at his locker, Mueller, still miffed that Mays had fielded balls that he thought should have been his, asked, "Hey, Willie, is it true you're the best center fielder in baseball?"

Mays, who felt he had only been following orders, didn't appreciate the remark. "The best right fielder, too," he answered.

Being quick of wit is not a prerequisite for playing center field, but being quick of foot is. More than any other position, center field demands speed—and Mays filled the bill. A few days after his exchange with Mueller, he made what may be the most famous catch in baseball history. It came during Game 1 of the 1954 World Series, with the Giants and the Cleveland Indians tied at 2–2 in the eighth inning. The Tribe's Larry Doby led off the top of the frame with a walk, then Al Rosen beat out an infield hit. That brought Vic Wertz to the plate. The left-handed slugger was already 3 for 3 against the Gi-

When you have outfielders with the speed of St. Louis' Willie McGee (5, opposite) and Vince Coleman, the problem isn't covering the gaps, but rather avoiding high-speed collisions. Center fielder McGee is a three-time Gold Glove winner.

The competition from other New York center fielders—the Yankees' Mickey Mantle and the Dodgers' Duke Snider—was intense in 1954, but the Giants' Willie Mays was at his best when in the spotlight. His leaping catch (right) took an extra-base hit away from Snider. "I believed when I went on that field that I was on stage," he said.

In 1987—his first full season in the majors—California right fielder Devon White led all AL outfielders in putouts with 424 to gain a title that usually goes to a center fielder. The Angels were so impressed that in 1988 they traded away four-time Gold Glove winner Gary Pettis and moved White to center.

ants' Sal Maglie, so Durocher called in left-handed reliever Don Liddle. Wertz had been pulling the ball all day, and Mays knew he'd be hitting behind the runners to try to advance them. So Mays shaded the batter to right field. He also suspected that Wertz would swing at the new pitcher's first offering. He was right.

"As soon as I picked [the ball] up in the sky, I knew I had to get over toward straightaway center field," said Mays, recalling the play. "I turned and ran full speed toward center with my back to the plate . . . about 450 feet away from the plate I looked over my shoulder and spotted the ball. I timed it perfectly and it dropped into my glove maybe 10 or 15 feet from the bleacher wall. At that same moment, I wheeled and threw in one motion and fell to the ground. I must have looked like a corkscrew. I could feel my hat flying off, but I saw the ball heading straight to Davey Williams on second." Williams caught the relay and threw home. Doby, who had tagged up at second, was held to third base, and Rosen scrambled to make it back to first. The catch was undoubtedly one of the most spectacular catches ever. And because it took place in a World Series, was witnessed by a national television audience and was captured dramatically in still photos, it is also one of the most famous catches in major league history.

But the "Say Hey Kid" made a number of equally breathtaking grabs. Two innings later in the same World Series game, Mays made another great play, and Wertz was again the victim. Marv Grissom was pitching for the Giants, and Wertz hit a screwball deep to left center. Mays was still playing Wertz toward right field, but he chased the ball, finally catching up to it after it bounced. He grabbed it bare-handed in the alley and threw it, turning what looked like a sure inside-the-park home run into a double.

Mays was playing minor league ball in Trenton in 1950 when Lou Haymen of Wilmington blasted a pitch to the 405-foot sign in dead center field. "I ran back, jumped, and caught it bare-handed just as it was going over," remembers Mays. "I bounced off the fence and threw the ball all the way on the fly to home plate."

That wasn't the last glove-free catch Mays would make. In 1951, his rookie year in the majors, Mays was playing center field in a game against the Pirates at Forbes Field. Pittsburgh first baseman Rocky Nelson, a left-handed hitter, smashed a pitch to dead center, 430 feet from home plate. Mays raced for the wall, but by the time he reached the warning track and looked over his shoulder, he saw that the ball was hooking to the right. Out of time to reach across his body and make the grab with his glove hand, he instinctively reached down with his bare hand and caught the ball at knee level.

Mays' teammate, the great Monte Irvin, remembers that everyone on the Giants' bench, including manager Durocher, was flabbergasted. "Nobody had ever seen anything like it," recalled Irvin. Durocher then decided to have a little fun with Mays, instructing his ballplayers to give the rookie the silent treatment when he came in at the end of the inning.

When Mays hit the dugout, nobody said a word. Mays waited for somebody to say something . . . and waited. Finally, he broke the silence himself. "Leo, didn't you see what I just did out there?"

But Durocher's lips remained buttoned.

"Leo," Mays repeated, "didn't you see what I did?"

Durocher finally turned around and looked at him, poker-faced. "No," he said, "I didn't see it. So you'll have to go out and do it again before I'll believe it."

No one has—or wants—more territory to cover than the center fielder. "You're in charge of the whole outfield," said former Blue Jays outfielder Bob Bailor. "You can run as far as you want, throw as far as you want . . . It's like you're a kid in your backyard again."

CESAR CEDENO
Outfield

6' 2" 175 lbs.
BR TR
b 2/25/1951

Cesar Cedeno's name belongs in any book about the fastest men in baseball. The Houston center fielder from the Dominican Republic stole more than 50 bases six years in a row from 1972 through 1977.

But his speed—on the basepaths and in the field—wasn't Cedeno's only talent. Close to flawless fielding won him five Gold Gloves. And he was usually solid at the plate, compiling a .285 lifetime average over his 17-year career.

Cedeno got off to a great start in the minors at 16. With a Kentucky team in the Appalachian League, Cedeno knocked out 49 hits in 36 games for a .374 average. Before the 1968 season was half over, the Astros moved Cedeno up to the Carolina League. By the end of the 1970 season, he was in the majors. In his first 90 games with the Astros, Cedeno hit .310 and showed talent on the bases, stealing 17 in 21 attempts.

In 1973 Astro manager Leo Durocher compared Cedeno to the best he ever coached—Willie Mays. Fans started calling the Astrodome "Cesar's Palace." Even when Cedeno slumped in 1977, manager Bill Virdon said, "He's still better at .179 than anybody else I could put in."

Late in the 1985 season, his last full year in the majors, Cedeno was traded to St. Louis. In 28 games, he hit .434 to help the Cardinals clinch the NL pennant.

At 5' 8" and around 200 pounds, Minnesota's Kirby Puckett is one of the game's most improbably constructed center fielders. But he's also one of the best. Puckett's specialty is reaching over fences to turn home runs into outs. He did it eight times in 1987.

But Pittsburgh's general manager, Branch Rickey, saw it. He sent a note to the Giants' dugout that read: "That was the finest catch I have ever seen and the finest catch I ever hope to see."

The finest throw Rickey might ever have hoped to see also took place that season on August 15, as the Giants began their remarkable run for the pennant. New York was playing first-place Brooklyn, and the score was tied, 1–1, with the Dodgers batting in the top of the eighth. With Billy Cox on third and Ralph Branca on first, the dangerous Carl Furillo came to the plate.

Furillo hit a catchable drive to right center, a hit that looked deep enough to drive home Cox with the go-ahead run. Mays, who had been playing the right-handed batter in left center, raced over and caught the ball running at full speed. For a moment, his back was to home plate. But in a flash he turned around and threw the ball home as Cox tagged up and took off for the plate. The ball buzzed toward cut-off man Whitey Lockman, who wisely watched it zip by. Catcher Wes Westrum gloved it on the fly and tagged out a surprised Cox. Westrum later estimated that the ball had been traveling 85 miles an hour—the speed of a good fastball—and that if it had been a pitch, it would have been a strike, "right over the heart of the plate." The Brooklyn rally was snuffed, and the Giants went on to win the game and the pennant on Bobby Thomson's "shot heard round the world."

While no one has ever calculated how much ground Mays covered chasing down hits over the course of his career, Bruce Nofziger, the groundskeeper at the California Angels' Anaheim Stadium, estimated that Gary Pettis, who played center for the Angels in the mid-1980s, defended 35,000 square feet of turf. That's about three-quarters of an

acre. Whether or not the left and right fielders are defensive liabilities on the order of Don Mueller, the center fielder is charged with covering balls hit into the gaps and backing up his fellow outfielders on balls hit to them. In *Playing the Field,* Jim Kaplan notes that center fielders are called upon to catch the ball as much as 25 percent more often than their outfield mates, and among outfielders they lead the majors in putouts most often.

Good center fielders are aggressive, and as a result sometimes pick up errors on balls other outfielders might not even get a glove on. But in 1985 Cleveland's Brett Butler played aggressive, nearly error-free center field, committing just one error in 457 total chances.

Yet the position has its advantages. Duke Snider, who played center for the Brooklyn Dodgers from 1947 to 1957, believed that center field was the easiest of the outfield positions. "You see the ball come off the bat better and it doesn't hook or slice as much as it does to left or right," he said. Perhaps this is the reason that center fielders are often the designated leaders in the outfield. Because they have a better view of the ball—one that is not obscured by batters on one side of the plate or the other —they can help out the other fielders by shouting stage directions. As the Red Sox' right fielder Dwight Evans says, "A center fielder who communicates well just by telling you 'Back! Back!' or 'In! In!' can mean the difference between plays made and not made."

Playing the wall is also less of a problem in center; fielders in left and right are forced to anticipate how the ball—or sometimes the fielder himself —is going to carom off the wall. And yet, one of the most promising center fielders of all time—Pete Reiser—ruined his career by colliding with the center field wall in Ebbets Field. Reiser played center for Brooklyn from 1940 to 1948. "The feeling about him in 1942," said the Braves' Tommy Holmes, "was that he was as great a star as there ever was in the game." Not only was he the youngest NL batting champion—he won the 1941 title at the age of 22

Continued on page 136

Arlington Stadium

Everything is bigger in Texas—except ball-parks. When the new home of the minor league Dallas-Fort Worth Spurs opened midway between the two cities, it was called Turnpike Stadium and held just 10,000 fans. Four expansions and one major league team later, Arlington Stadium—renamed after the Washington Senators moved to Texas and became the Rangers in 1972—was still the AL's second-smallest park, with a capacity of 43,508. Only Boston's Fenway Park is smaller.

But for the Rangers' first two seasons, the size of the stadium didn't seem to matter. The team drew fewer than 700,000 fans and lost at least 100 games both years. Things started on a hopeful note in the Rangers' inaugural home game on April 21, 1972, as slugger Frank Howard blasted a first-inning homer in a 7–6 win over the Angels. But a strong wind that blew in from the outfield frustrated Ranger sluggers, who hit just 33 of the 74 homers in Arlington Stadium that season. Since it was a pitcher's park, it was only fitting that the stadium's first capacity crowd came out to see a pitcher—18-year-old southpaw David Clyde. Clyde, a bonus baby just graduated from a Houston high school, allowed one hit and struck out eight in five innings before a sellout crowd of 35,694 on June 27, 1973. But the young fireballer never lived up to expectations, and was 7–18 in three seasons with the Rangers. Later that season the stadium became one hitter's landmark when the Indians' Frank Robinson homered on September 19, making Arlington the 32nd park in which he had homered, a major league record.

In 1974 manager Billy Martin—hired near the end of the 1973 season—guided the Rangers to an 84–76 record, a 27-game improvement over their previous season, and second place in the AL West. Right fielder Jeff Burroughs turned in an MVP season, pitcher Ferguson Jenkins won 25 games and was named Comeback Player of the Year, and attendance topped one million. Except for the strike-shortened 1981 season, the Rangers have drawn over a million every year since, but have remained one of baseball's most inconsistent teams. From 1972 through 1989 they finished second five times, last five times, and had 13 managers.

The Rangers have traditionally been a good running team, with base-stealers like Bump Wills—son of Maury Wills—Bert Campaneris, Dave Nelson, Lenny Randle and Billy Sample. The team led the AL in steals in its rookie year, and in 1978 set a club record with 196.

In 1985, however, the focus shifted from speed to power when a high wall was built around the outfield fences, thereby cutting the wind. A record 178 home runs were hit at Arlington that season, 76 by the Rangers. The power surge reached a peak in 1987, when the Rangers—with young sluggers like Ruben Sierra and Pete Incaviglia and veterans Pete O'Brien and Larry Parrish—hit a team record 194 home runs, 93 at home.

In 1984 Arlington Stadium's two most noteworthy pitching feats took place, though neither was turned in by a Ranger pitcher. On July 4, 45-year-old Yankee knuckleballer Phil Niekro became just the ninth pitcher in history to strike out 3,000 batters. On September 30, Angel curveballer Mike Witt—21 years Niekro's junior—closed out the season with a perfect game.

In case you forget what state you're in, the scoreboard at Arlington Stadium (above) provides an instant reminder. And while the Rangers play in one of baseball's hottest climates, it's also one of the driest. In their first 18 years at Arlington Stadium, the Rangers were rained out just 37 times, and twice went entire seasons without a rainout.

Arlington Stadium

1700 Copeland Avenue,
Arlington, Texas

Built 1964

Texas Rangers, AL
  1972-present

Seating Capacity
43,508

Style
Minor League Expanded

Height of Outfield Fences
11 feet

Dugouts
Home: 1st base
Visitor: 3rd base

Bullpens
Foul Territory
Home: Right field
Visitor: Left field

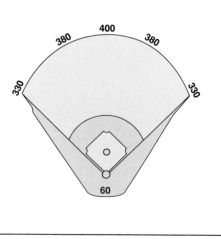

The biggest problem Fred Lynn (above, leaping over Carl Yastrzemski) has in center field is avoiding other outfielders and outfield walls. The injury-prone Lynn has won four Gold Gloves, but through 1989 had played more than 140 games in a season just four times in his 16-year career.

with a .343 average—but he was spectacular on defense. He combined athletic ability with a certain amount of reckless abandon in chasing down balls, resulting in some of the most spectacular catches ever. He was so reckless that he often injured himself, and, according to one sportswriter of the time, was carried off the field a total of 11 times in his career. But Reiser went on to spend the war years in the service, and when he returned to Ebbets Field in 1946, the wall had been moved in nearly 40 feet. In a 1947 game in Brooklyn, Reiser was chasing down a Pirate hit with typical abandon and he crashed into the wall so hard that he was knocked unconscious—but he didn't drop the ball. Reiser was carried from the field and remained unconscious for ten days. He recovered enough to play on and off for another five years, but never regained his form.

By virtue of the ground he has to cover, a center fielder must have both quickness and speed. Excellent timing, a quick first step and good range—having the speed to cover a lot of turf—are essential.

It isn't surprising that a long line of talented athletes have manned the position since the late 19th century, among them Bill Lange, Ty Cobb, Tris Speaker, Max Carey, Cool Papa Bell and Oscar Charleston of the Negro leagues, Terry Moore, Joe and Dom DiMaggio, Richie Ashburn, Willie Mays and Mickey Mantle, Curt Flood, Paul Blair, Fred Lynn, Andre Dawson, Dale Murphy and Andy Van Slyke.

Perhaps the least known of the group, Lange was one of the greatest athletes to play major league baseball in the 19th century. He played for the Chicago Colts—who later became the Cubs—from 1893 through 1899. Nicknamed "Little Eva," he was big for his day: about 6'2" and 200 pounds. But he also had speed. In 811 games he stole 399 bases, leading the league with

Mickey Mantle (left) inherited the spacious center field at Yankee Stadium from Joe DiMaggio, perhaps the smoothest outfielder ever to play there. Mantle's style was chaotic—but effective. With Mantle, said second baseman Gil McDougald, "Every catch was a sensational one. First, he'd misjudge the ball. Then he'd outrun it. Finally, he'd catch it. It was like watching two movies at the same time."

73 in 1897. Even though the stolen base was scored differently in those days, Lange's totals put him near the top of base-stealers of his time, and the comments of writers of the era suggest that he may have been the fastest player of the 1890s.

Lange won praise for his hitting—he batted .389 in 1895 and .330 for his career—but he drew even greater raves for his fielding. Some of the catches he made were remarkable. But one catch, if it actually took place, stands far above the rest. Legend has it that in a game at Washington, the Colts were leading, 6–5, in the bottom of the 11th inning. Washington's Kip Selbach, an excellent hitter, came to the plate with two out and a runner on base. Selbach hit a line drive to deep center and had a sure extra-base hit, but, the story goes, Lange came from nowhere, diving, somersaulting, literally crashing through the fence. A few moments passed, then Lange reappeared through the splintered fence, ball in hand, having saved the game for the Colts.

Baseball historian Arthur Ahrens says the story is pure myth. He points out that none of the papers chronicling Chicago-Washington games of the period ever mentioned such a remarkable feat. The game that came closest probably took place on August 31, 1896. On that day, in the tenth inning of a scoreless game in Washington, Chicago first baseman George Decker broke his wrist and had to leave the game. The left field fence was apparently adjacent to a hospital, so Washington's Selbach walked Decker to the fence, grabbed a ladder and used it like a battering ram to shatter the fence and create a shortcut for Decker. Later in the inning, with a runner on third and two out, Washington's Gene Demontreville hit a low liner to left center. The *Washington Post* reporter covering the game wrote, "[Lange] stumbled and

Today's speedy, shallow-playing center fielders are just picking up where Tris Speaker left off. Speaker played so shallow that in April 1918 he turned two unassisted double plays. "I have found it best to be on hand for the short hits and to take a chance on the long ones," he said.

5' 11½" 165 lbs.   b 4/26/1947
BR TR

AMOS OTIS
Outfield

When Amos Otis broke into the majors at age 20, his greatest ambition was not to embarrass himself. Hailing from Mobile, Alabama—hometown of Billy Williams, Willie McCovey and Hank Aaron—Otis had big shoes to fill.

Otis was, for a time, the fastest man in baseball, having been clocked at 3.6 seconds from home to first—about two steps better than the average right-handed batter. In 1970 he stole 33 bases for Kansas City and was thrown out only twice; in 1971 his 52 steals led the AL. And although he hit .300 and 26 homers in 1973, Otis remained modest: "Whenever I hit a home run I'm as surprised as everybody else."

But the center fielder was even better on defense. His great speed allowed him to cover the lion's share of the outfield at Royals Stadium, the AL's first artificial-surface ballpark. And his patented one-handed catches were no liability: he once went 165 games without an error, twice led AL outfielders in chances, putouts and double plays, and was a three-time Gold Glove winner.

But age creeps up on speedsters more suddenly than other ballplayers. At 36, after 16 years in the majors, Otis violated Satchel Paige's credo, "Never look back." Always measuring himself against the best, Otis said in 1983, "I can look back and see the fastest man in baseball coming up on me." And like a runner in a relay race, Otis was forced to pass the baton to teammate Willie Wilson and watch him go by.

Andre Dawson is solid gold no matter where he plays. Dawson won four straight Gold Gloves in center with the Expos from 1980 to 1983, then moved to right and won four more, two with Montreal in 1984 and 1985 and two with the Cubs in 1987 and 1988.

lost his balance and fell, but clung to the ball. From the grandstand it looked like Lange covered almost half the distance spanned by the ball." As time passed, the natural tendency to embellish athletic accomplishments probably did turn Lange's great catch of Demontreville's drive into the unbelievable fence-busting grab of Selbach's smash.

Yet Lange made enough documented great catches to make almost any story credible. And Albert Spalding—famed pitcher, baseball historian and sporting goods manufacturer—chose Lange for his all-time all-star outfield over Tris Speaker. Wrote Spalding: "Both men could go back or to either side equally well. Both were lightning fast in handling ground balls. But no man I ever saw could go forward and get a low line drive like Lange."

Despite Spalding's choice, it is Hall of Famer Speaker, not Lange, who almost always runs one-two with Willie Mays when the experts rate the best-ever defensive center fielders. Speaker played for the Boston Red Sox from 1907 to 1915, spent 11 seasons with the Cleveland Indians, played a year in Washington and then finished his career in 1928 with the Philadelphia Athletics. One of the fastest players of his day, he is credited with revolutionizing center field play by challenging the idea that the center fielder must play deep and keep the ball in front of him. He believed that it made more sense to give up an occasional extra-base hit to cut down on the number of singles falling in front of him. He played so shallow that he was actually able to complete a record four unassisted double plays, and he still holds the major league records for double plays, with 139, and assists, with 448, and is second to Mays in putouts by an outfielder with 6,791. His numbers are all the more remarkable because Speaker, a natural right-hander,

became a left-hander after falling off a horse and breaking his right arm at the age of ten.

Speaker's former teammate, pitching great Smoky Joe Wood, said of him: "He had that terrific instinct—at the crack of the bat he'd be off with his back to the infield, and then he'd turn and glance over his shoulder at the last minute and catch the ball so easy it looked like there was nothing to it, nothing at all. Nobody else was even in the same league with him."

In addition to instinct, Speaker had smarts. He was widely considered one of the most intelligent ballplayers of his era. At Boston, he and catcher Bill Carrigan conspired to trick slow-thinking base-stealers. As a stealer headed for second, Speaker ran in and Carrigan intentionally overthrew the ball into center field. As the unwitting runner picked himself up and headed for third, Speaker one-hopped the ball and threw it to the base ahead of the runner.

Unlike Mays, Speaker was blessed with excellent mates in the outfield. Between 1910 and 1915, Speaker, right fielder Harry Hooper and left fielder Duffy Lewis formed what many historians consider to be the best outfield in history. Hooper, who batted a respectable .281 over his career, is one of the few players elected to the Hall of Fame because of their defensive skills. He invented the "rump slide"—the now-popular skidding catch of short fly balls. Lewis so mastered a ten-foot incline in left field at the new Fenway Park in 1912 that it was named "Duffy's Cliff" after him.

Speaker was, without a doubt, the best major league center fielder of his time. But he may have been given a run for the money as the top center

Detroit's Gary Pettis (above, center) is so fast that he's almost always in perfect position to throw after making the catch. And he makes lots of catches. In 1985 Pettis tied a major league record with 12 putouts in one game.

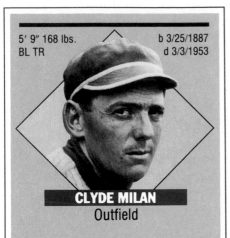

CLYDE MILAN
Outfield

5' 9" 168 lbs.
BL TR

b 3/25/1887
d 3/3/1953

Washington Senators catcher Cliff Blankenship will always be remembered for the 1907 Midwestern scouting trip on which he discovered pitching star Walter Johnson. But often forgotten is the original purpose of that trip: to sign center fielder Jesse Clyde "Deerfoot" Milan. Milan played 16 seasons with the Senators, had a .285 career average and stole 495 bases, making him 17th on the all-time list.

Milan did not hit well in his first three years in Washington, but his fielding kept him in the lineup. He played shallower in center field than Tris Speaker but could still outrun drives deep to the outfield.

Milan was a contact hitter with an excellent on-base percentage of .388. In 1911 Milan's batting average surged to .315, and he took advantage of his frequent visits to first base by stealing 58 bases.

The next year Milan had his best season on the basepaths and snatched the stolen-base crown from Ty Cobb. He stole 88 bases, including five in the course of three innings against Cleveland on June 14.

Milan repeated as league leader in 1913 with 75, the last year his batting average topped .300 and his steals topped 40. He retired as a player after the 1922 season, and later became a coach for the Senators. During a 1953 spring training practice, while Milan hit to outfielders in 80-degree heat, he suffered a fatal heart attack.

Duke Snider (above, left) had as much speed and athletic talent as his New York center field rivals—Willie Mays and Mickey Mantle—but had to be more careful in his outfield sprints because of the close-in concrete walls at Brooklyn's Ebbets Field.

fielder in baseball by Oscar Charleston, a Negro league great who broke into baseball in 1915. Charleston, called both "the Black Ty Cobb" and "the Black Tris Speaker," combined the aggressiveness of Cobb with the grace of Speaker. Blessed with great speed, he positioned himself as shallow as Speaker did and was able to run back and catch balls that, say his contemporaries, Willie Mays would have had a hard time reaching. Although he was too old to play in the major leagues when the color barrier was finally broken, he was elected to the Hall of Fame in 1976.

One of Speaker's contemporaries, Max Carey, was, in the eyes of many, the best NL center fielder ever until Mays came along. Carey preyed on balls hit his way from 1910 to 1926 with the Pittsburgh Pirates, and from 1926 to 1929 with the Brooklyn Dodgers. He led the NL in putouts nine of those seasons and held the career putout record for center fielders until Lloyd Waner broke it. Eventually, Mays captured the record. But Carey's 339 assists still rank as tops in post-1900 league history for an outfielder.

Carey was one of the fastest men of his era, and at a field day in Cincinnati is said to have tied Hans Lobert's record of 13.8 seconds around the bases. He ranks fifth on the all-time stolen-base list with 738, led the league ten times and in 1922 stole 51 bases in 53 tries. Age didn't seem to slow him down, either. He stole second, third and home in the same inning twice: once at age 33, once at 35. In 1925 he enjoyed one of the best World Series ever. Playing with a broken rib, he still managed to steal three bases and bat .458. In Game 7, he tallied four hits off the great Walter Johnson to lead the Pirates to victory and the championship.

After the Speaker-Cobb-Charleston-Carey era, it was nearly 20 years until as many celebrated center fielders surfaced at the same time. In the in-

At the plate, Boston's Dom DiMaggio wasn't nearly the equal of his older brother Joe, but in center field the family resemblance was obvious. In 1948 Dom became the first AL outfielder in history to top 500 putouts in a season, and his mark of 503 stood until Chet Lemon broke it in 1977.

Joe DiMaggio covered Yankee Stadium's cavernous center field with long strides and flawless judgment. "He never seemed to be in a hurry, but he was always there," said Giants outfielder Monte Irvin.

terim, the best defensive center fielder was the Cardinals' Terry Moore, who played from 1935 to 1948. Moore not only made some of the most spectacular catches ever, he also led the league in fielding percentage once, putouts twice and total chances three times. In a 1936 game against the Giants, he made a sliding basket catch—bare-handed—to rob Mel Ott of a hit. In the 1942 World Series, he made a spectacular catch of a Joe DiMaggio hit that some say must have sailed at least 485 feet from the plate before Moore snatched it out of the air. "It seemed like I ran a full minute before I caught up with the ball," Moore said. "I had my back to the infield, caught the ball over my shoulder, and then almost hit the fence." The DiMaggio brothers also earned high marks for their glovework. Bostonians used to joke that Ted Williams should give little Dom DiMaggio a not-so-little portion of his paycheck because of the balls he caught in left center field. And because Joe was such a dominant offensive player, people often forget that he did a superb job of patrolling "Death Valley"—the vast center field in Yankee Stadium. In 51 World Series games he made only one error. And in his final Series, he chased down a hard-hit line drive off the bat of the Giants' rookie center fielder, Willie Mays. On the same play, Yankee rookie and right fielder Mickey Mantle injured his knee trying to back DiMaggio up.

By the following season, DiMaggio had retired, Mantle had moved over to center, and he and Mays—along with Brooklyn's Duke Snider—were contending in the greatest center field rivalry of all time. The only city ever to have three major league teams, New York also seemed to have cornered the market on great center fielders. For pure speed, Mantle—when he wasn't injured—was the leader. Mays was the acrobat, whirling and spinning his way across the spacious center field at New York's Polo Grounds. Snider may

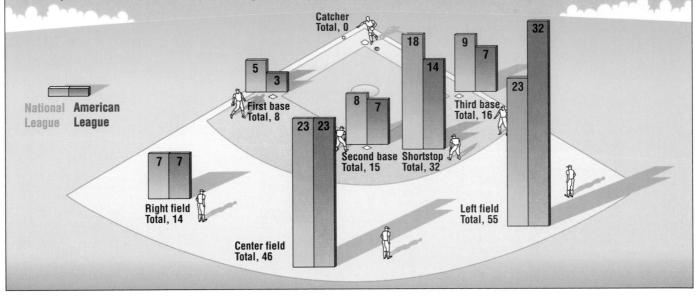

Speed by Position

Where do the top base–stealers play defense? Logic says up the middle—shortstop, second base and center field—and to a certain extent that's the case. Center fielders—led by Ty Cobb and Max Carey—have won 45 league base–stealing titles since 1901. Shortstops have won 32, but almost half belong to Luis Aparicio and Bert Campaneris. Left-fielders lead the way with 55, thanks largely to the NL's Lou Brock, Tim Raines and Vince Coleman—who combined for 20 titles. No catcher has ever won a base-stealing title. Below are the totals of league base-stealing champs, by position, from 1901 to 1991.

National League   American League

Catcher Total, 0

First base Total, 8 — 5 · 3

Second base Total, 15 — 8 · 7 · 23 · 23

Shortstop Total, 32 — 18 · 14

Third base Total, 16 — 9 · 7 · 23

Left field Total, 55 — 32

Right field Total, 14 — 7 · 7

Center field Total, 46 — 23 · 23

have been the best all-around athlete of the three; he lettered in baseball, basketball, football and track in high school. He could run with the other two and had a tremendous arm: Stan Musial called the Brooklyn trio of Snider, Andy Pafko and Carl Furillo "the best-throwing outfield I ever saw."

As the 1950s progressed, Willie Mays, Mickey Mantle and Duke Snider became the prototypes for the center fielder—power hitters who combined speed in the field with strong throwing arms. But with the building of big new artificial-surface stadiums, the nature of the job description for center field has changed. No longer can the confident center fielder play on the edge of the infield, trying to prevent hits. Because lined shots can skip off the rug in left and right center and shoot to the wall, he must play back to cut off balls that are already hits. A handful of rifle-armed sluggers still cover center —Atlanta's Dale Murphy, for one—but it is more often the snipers like Brett Butler, Lenny Dykstra and Jerome Walton who stand where Willie, Mickey and the Duke once stood. ◗❚

An eight-time Gold Glove winner, center fielder Paul Blair (opposite) anchored an Oriole defense that was a key to five division titles and four pennants from 1966 to 1974.

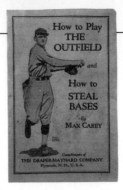

Max Carey

Most ballplayers who hit .158 in their first minor league season wind up finding other lines of work. Not Max Carey. He wound up in the Hall of Fame. By the time Carey retired in 1929, he had stolen more bases and caught more fly balls and line drives than anyone else in the history of the National League. It was 40 years before Willie Mays broke his record for putouts by an outfielder and 45 before Lou Brock broke his record for stolen bases. But Carey had neither the natural talent of Mays nor the raw speed of Brock. He was a self-made star, one whose achievements "were the results of long and patient effort, of rigid self-analysis," according to sportswriter F. C. Lane. If Carey had a gift, it was his ability to teach himself by watching others.

Carey's first important lesson on the road to Cooperstown came when he was 13. Enrolled by his parents in a six-year preparatory course at Concordia College, a Lutheran seminary in Indiana, Carey was beaten in a race by a classmate he thought to be "particularly ungainly and awkward." So the young minister-to-be started watching the school's best sprinter and pretty soon had a slew of track medals of his own. Carey also played baseball at Concordia, and the summer after he graduated he attended a Central League game between South Bend and Terre Haute. Convinced he was better than the South Bend shortstop, he approached the team's manager, with track medals in hand, and offered his services. He dropped his real name, Maximilian Carnarius, and began his professional baseball career the next day under the name Max Carey. He hit poorly and committed 24 errors in 48 games. Only his speed got him a return invitation to the team in 1910.

In the off-season Carey worked on his game. A natural right-hander, he became a switch-hitter to take advantage of his speed. He was moved to the outfield at the start of the season, hit .293 and was purchased by the Pittsburgh Pirates in August. He played for the Pirates for the next 16 years and, under the tutelage of Hall of Famer Honus Wagner, quickly became the NL's stolen-base king. Wagner led the NL in steals five times, but his pupil was twice as good—winning a record ten stolen-base titles from 1913 to 1925. In 1922 he stole 51 bases and was thrown out only twice—both times on a hit-and-run in which the batter swung and missed—for an all-time record success rate of 96.2 percent.

Carey approached stealing bases as studiously and methodically as he did the rest of his game. While Ty Cobb was terrorizing the AL with his flashing spikes and intimidating style, Carey was driving NL opponents crazy with quiet, unrelenting efficiency. He was a master at studying the motions of pitchers and timing his takeoff perfectly. "I never pay the slightest attention to the catcher," he wrote. "I know if I can get a proper start, the greatest catcher who ever lived cannot prevent me from stealing second. All my attention is centered rather on the pitcher. He is the man I have to outwit and if I can do so, the catcher does not count in my calculations."

Carey took the longest lead in baseball and, as a result, spent a lot of time and energy diving back to first. Cardinal pitcher Jesse Haines once threw to first 17 times trying to wear Carey out, but Carey had a few tricks of his own. "It is surprising how long it takes a base-stealer to lace his shoes when he wants to get his wind," he wrote. And besides, he was flattered by all the attention. "When I am on first if a pitcher doesn't favor me with half a dozen throws I think I am being neglected."

As an outfielder, Carey was almost without peer. His speed helped him cover the huge power al-

Max Carey went after fly balls and line drives better than just about anyone who ever played center field—even Tris Speaker. Carey averaged at least three chances per game nine times in his career, compared with five times for Speaker.

leys in Pittsburgh's Forbes Field, and he led the NL in putouts nine times, a major league record equaled only by Richie Ashburn. But just as he was overshadowed as a base-stealer by Cobb, it was Carey's misfortune to play at the same time as Cleveland's Tris Speaker, considered by many to be the greatest outfielder ever. But in 1912 Carey set a major league record for left fielders with 369 putouts, then five years later set the center field record with 440. According to *Baseball Magazine,* "for ability to cover ground, to catch the greatest number of balls, to handle the greatest number of chances over a long period of time, it is very doubtful if the game has yet seen Max Carey's equal."

But he saved his hardest work for his hitting, because it came the toughest. He topped .300 six times in his career but also had seasons of .231, .243 and .254. "I was not naturally a hitter," Carey admitted. "Far from it." But midway through his career he found his stroke, and from 1919 to 1925 he hit .300 four times, hitting .289 and .297 the other two years. In 1925, at 35, Carey made another change. After watching Ty Cobb hit, he adopted Cobb's style and separated his hands on the bat. He hit a career-high .343, and wound up playing in his first World Series, where he turned in the most celebrated—and perhaps the smartest—performance of his career.

The Pirates lost three of the first four games to the defending world-champion Washington Senators, and in Game 5 Carey suffered two broken ribs. Corseted but undaunted, Carey scored a crucial run in a 3–2 Pirate win in Game 6, then let it all hang out in Game 7. Somehow Carey discovered that Walter Johnson, the Senators' Game 7 starter, was tipping off his pitches. Whether he coaxed the news out of a Senators player who was sure Johnson would not pitch again in the Series, or figured it out on his own, depends on whose story you believe. In any case, the Pirates, who had managed just 11 hits against Johnson in Games 1 and 4, pounded the Big Train for 15 in Game 7. Carey led the charge with four hits—three of them doubles—three runs scored and two RBI as the Pirates won, 9–7, in one of the wildest Series finales ever. Carey wound up the top hitter in the Series at .458 and stole three bases to boot.

Carey was put on waivers by the Pirates in 1926. A year later he returned—as a Brooklyn Dodger—to Forbes Field, where fans had never cared that he wasn't Ty Cobb or Tris Speaker. Their welcome brought tears to Carey's eyes. "There came from the Forbes Field stands and bleachers an outburst of cheering as had not smitten the Schenley suburbs for many a year," read one newspaper report. "They saluted him for fully five minutes. Carey faced the pitcher, then stepped out of the batter's box, presumably to pry a pebble out of his spikes."

Carey managed the Dodgers in 1932 and 1933, and stayed in baseball as a coach, scout and manager until 1956. When, at age 71, he was inducted into the Hall of Fame, he had still stolen more bases and caught more fly balls and line drives than anyone else in the history of the National League.

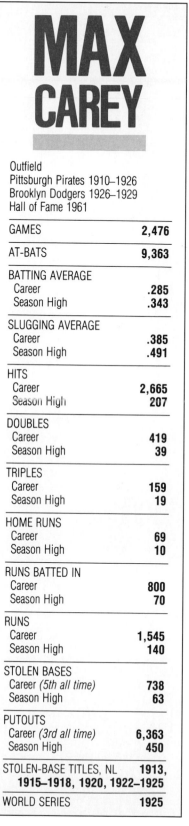

MAX
CAREY

Outfield
Pittsburgh Pirates 1910–1926
Brooklyn Dodgers 1926–1929
Hall of Fame 1961

GAMES	**2,476**
AT-BATS	**9,363**
BATTING AVERAGE	
Career	**.285**
Season High	**.343**
SLUGGING AVERAGE	
Career	**.385**
Season High	**.491**
HITS	
Career	**2,665**
Season High	**207**
DOUBLES	
Career	**419**
Season High	**39**
TRIPLES	
Career	**159**
Season High	**19**
HOME RUNS	
Career	**69**
Season High	**10**
RUNS BATTED IN	
Career	**800**
Season High	**70**
RUNS	
Career	**1,545**
Season High	**140**
STOLEN BASES	
Career *(5th all time)*	**738**
Season High	**63**
PUTOUTS	
Career *(3rd all time)*	**6,363**
Season High	**450**
STOLEN-BASE TITLES, NL	**1913,**
1915–1918, 1920, 1922–1925	
WORLD SERIES	**1925**

The Redbird Express

Sliding headfirst into first base was the way St. Louis' Frankie Frisch played the game, especially during the World Series. In the 1930 Series against the Athletics, Frisch's single in Game 2 gave him 43 career Series hits, moving him ahead of Eddie Collins into first place on the all-time list. He ended his career with 58 Series hits, and was passed by Yogi Berra in 1958.

Pepper Martin typified the Cardinals' all-out style of play in the 1930s. Cincinnati first baseman Frank McCormick (preceding page) stretched in vain as Martin hustled out a hit in a 1939 game.

While baseball in the lively-ball era rarely involved the bunt and the stolen base, speed and aggressiveness did remain important for a number of pennant winners between 1920 and 1960. In 1921 John McGraw's champion New York Giants ran the basepaths with the daring, if not the abandon, they had in the dead-ball days. And in 1959 the Go Go White Sox topped the American League even though they were the only club in either league to hit fewer than 100 home runs.

But during those 40 years, the St. Louis Cardinals won more than their fair share of pennants by relying on hustle. From the Depression to post-World War II, the Cards proved that inside baseball still had a place in the game, from Pepper Martin's five steals in the 1931 World Series to Enos Slaughter's racing from first base to score the deciding run in the final game of the 1946 Series against Boston.

Nineteen thirty was, perhaps, the liveliest offensive year in baseball history. With the Great Depression at its worst and wallets close to empty, the powers that be—team owners—figured that more hitting power would put people in the seats, so they juiced up the ball. The results were astonishing. In 1930 no fewer than nine teams achieved a club batting average of .300; the entire National League average was .303. Since 1937, only one team has hit over .300. In 1930 the Cubs' Hack Wilson also became the first player to challenge Babe Ruth's home run record, and although he fell four short of 60, he did drive in an all-time-high 190 runs. In winning the National League pennant that year, all eight Cardinal starters batted over .300, while the team stole only 72 bases—still the second best in the league.

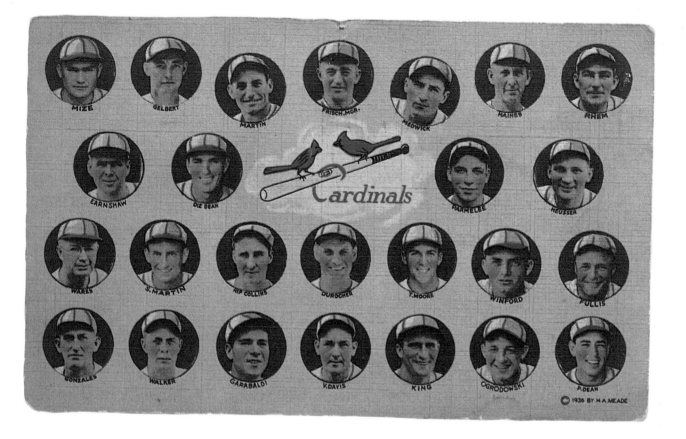

But the rabbit ball lost some of its liveliness in 1931. And with a change in the ball came a change in the Cards' style of play. St. Louis hit only 60 home runs, 44 fewer than the previous year, and speed and defense assumed greater prominence. Considered the most daring running team in the league, the 1931 Cardinals stole a league-leading 114 bases. Second baseman Frankie Frisch, who had stolen 15 bases in 1930, was the league champ with 28. In all, the Cards boasted four of the league's top five base-stealers.

Frisch, "the Fordham Flash," was the closest thing to a superstar on the squad. A fiery competitor with a hot temper, he had been a protégé of Giants manager John McGraw until the two began feuding in 1924. The feud started when McGraw wrote a guest column for a New York newspaper. In the column, McGraw criticized Frisch, whom the players had recently named team captain: "Frisch, by being given free rein, developed an individuality that proved to be a detriment to the teamwork of my other players," wrote the manager. The matter came to a head in 1926, during a game against the Cardinals in St. Louis. With Cardinal runners on first and third, McGraw suspected a double steal and signaled his catcher to fake the throw to second and to throw to the pitcher instead, in an effort to catch the runner off third. Since there would be no throw to second, neither the shortstop nor the second baseman needed to cover the base. But Frisch apparently missed the sign. The Cardinals did attempt the steal, and Frisch moved to cover second base. Cardinals batter Tommy Thevenow tapped a slow grounder to the spot Frisch had vacated, and what would normally have been an easy out became an RBI single. When the Giants returned to the dugout, McGraw exploded at Frisch, calling him a "dumb Dutchman" and a "cement head." Frisch left the

In 1936 the Cardinals still featured most of the same players that had won a world title in 1934—Leo Durocher, Frankie Frisch, Pepper Martin, Ducky Medwick and Dizzy Dean—and had added slugging first baseman Johnny Mize. But except for Dean, the pitching staff was thin, and the Cards finished third.

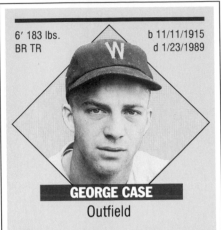

6' 183 lbs.   b 11/11/1915
BR TR   d 1/23/1989

GEORGE CASE

Outfield

"He's the most dangerous one-run man in the league," said White Sox manager Jimmy Dykes. "I tell my pitchers, first thing, 'keep Case off base.' "

The Senators' George Case spent 11 seasons unnerving American League pitchers, winning five straight stolen-base crowns from 1939 through 1943. His career high of 61 in 1943 was not bettered in the major leagues until Maury Wills 'stole a record-breaking 104 bases in 1962.

Case spent two seasons with a minor league club in Trenton, New Jersey, where his .338 batting average and the fact that he had beaten out 25 of 27 attempted bunts impressed Washington scouts. He was brought up at the end of the 1937 season, and former Senators speedster Clyde Milan was called in as his personal coach.

Case became so renowned for his running that he often ran publicity races against other athletes. While playing for Cleveland in 1946, Case took part in owner Bill Veeck's first big promotion stunt, a race against Olympic gold medalist Jesse Owens. It was Case's only loss.

Case also shone in the field and with the bat. He led AL outfielders in assists in 1941 and in a 1940 doubleheader got nine hits in ten at-bats to tie a major league record.

A back injury cut short Case's career in 1947 when he was 31. While his 349 steals rank him only 48th on the all-time list, his average of 44 steals per 154-game season matches greats like Ty Cobb and Bert Campaneris.

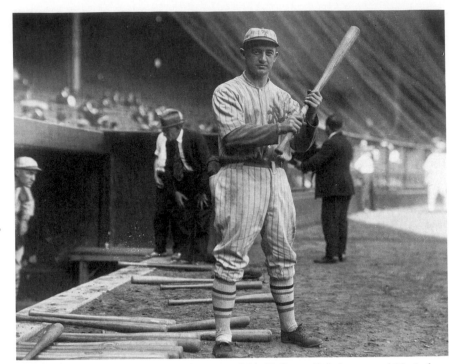

Playing in New York under Giants manager John McGraw, Frisch averaged 30 steals a season from 1920 to 1926. Being traded to St. Louis didn't slow him down much, as he averaged 29 steals in his first five seasons with the Cards.

team after the game and stayed away for the rest of the road trip. He did return when the team got back to New York, but was traded at the end of the season to St. Louis for Rogers Hornsby, a move McGraw had said he would never make.

Frisch enjoyed several fine seasons in St. Louis. In 1931 he batted .311, knocked in 82 runs and was named the league's Most Valuable Player. But the Cards were far from a one-man team that season. Rookie Pepper Martin and first basemen Jim Bottomley and Ripper Collins each hit .300 or better, and outfielder Chick Hafey won the league batting championship, edging out the Giants' Bill Terry, .3489 to .3486.

In becoming the first National League team to win more than 100 games in the home run era, the Cards spent all but three days of the season in first place. Still, Connie Mack's Philadelphia Athletics were favored in the World Series. The A's, who had posted a 107–45 record, boasted stars such as Lefty Grove, Jimmie Foxx, Mickey Cochrane and Al Simmons, who led the majors that year with a .390 batting average.

But the Cardinals, led by Martin, were an aggressive bunch. One of the game's most colorful characters, Martin sat on the Cards' bench until mid-July, when he confronted general manager Branch Rickey. "I want to get into the game—or I want you to trade me to some club that will play me," the brash young man said. Realizing Martin's potential, Rickey traded starting center fielder Taylor Douthit—who was hitting .331 at the time—to make room in the lineup for the rookie. Martin didn't disappoint Rickey, or his teammates. He batted an even .300 and stole 16 bases—third best in the league. But it was in the seven World Series games against the mighty

Athletics that he established his reputation. In Game 1 he had a double and two singles and he stole a base off the A's talented catcher, Cochrane. But the other Cardinal bats were silent, and the A's won, 6–2. St. Louis won Game 2, 2–0, behind the pitching of Bill Hallahan. Again, Martin provided all the offense, playing a brand of baseball that had been largely forgotten for more than a decade. In the second inning, he stretched a single into a double with a belly slide, stole third and scored on a sacrifice fly. In the seventh inning, he singled, stole second, moved to third on an infield out and dived home on a squeeze bunt.

Martin's showmanship continued as the Series moved from St. Louis to Philadelphia. In Game 3 Martin went 2 for 4 against Grove and scored two runs in a Cardinals' victory. In Game 4 he stole another base and got the only two Cardinal hits in a 3–0 loss. In Game 5 Martin had three hits, including a home run, and he batted in four of his club's five runs to lead them to a 5–1 victory.

Having almost single-handedly run and batted his team to a 3–2 Series lead, Martin cooled off at the plate. He was hitless in Game 6—won 8–1 by the A's—and in Game 7. In the final contest he did steal a base, but it was his running, juggling catch of a ball hit to left center with two outs in the ninth—the Cards ahead, 4–2, and the tying runs on base—that ended the Series. In all, he went 12 for 24 with four doubles, a home run and five steals.

After the game, baseball Commissioner Kenesaw Mountain Landis told Martin, "Young man, I'd rather trade places with you than any man in the country."

Martin smiled and said, "Why that'll be fine, Judge, if we can trade salaries, too."

For Cardinal outfielder Ernie Orsatti—who was a Hollywood stuntman in the off-season—hurling his body to the ground in the World Series was no problem. Orsatti's triple gave the Cards a 1–0 lead over the Tigers in Game 2 of the 1934 Series, but Goose Goslin's single in the 12th gave Detroit a 3–2 win.

Joe "Ducky" Medwick was a one-man offense for the Cardinals in the 1934 World Series. In his first four at-bats in Game 1 against Detroit, Medwick (right, scoring) had three singles and a home run. He wound up the Series hitting .379, and the Cardinals beat the Tigers in seven games.

Martin was still in the Cardinals' lineup, not the commissioner's office, when the Cards returned to the World Series in 1934. With Martin stealing a league-leading 23 bases, the Cards topped the NL in steals—with a paltry 69—as they had every season since 1931. But it was the team's overall aggressive style of play—its dirty uniforms, its headfirst slides—that earned it the nickname, "the Gashouse Gang." Second baseman Frisch was also the team's manager, and the spirit with which he played the game carried throughout the roster. Outfielder Joe "Ducky" Medwick, who had joined the team in 1932, and shortstop Leo "the Lip" Durocher, who arrived in 1933, were as aggressive on the bases as their boss, and rookie catcher Bill DeLancey was an equally tough competitor. In one game, Cards' pitching great Dizzy Dean had a big lead and appeared to be loafing on the mound. DeLancey whipped the ball back to him harder than Dean had thrown it, and then ran out to the mound himself. "If you ever throw any of that crap again when I'm catching, I'll knock you right on your seat," said the catcher.

Dean and his brother Paul accounted for 49 of the Cards' 95 wins, as the team won the pennant by two games over the Giants. Dizzy had 30 wins in 1934, a remarkable record for the lively-ball era. It remained the best single-season performance for a pitcher until 1968, when it was broken by Denny McLain with 31 wins. Dizzy's nickname was apt; he was as lively as the ball itself. He once gave out three different birthdates and birthplaces to three different writers on the same day, later explaining that he wanted each writer to have his own unique story.

Dean's dizziness was rivaled by that of his teammates—Durocher, pitcher Dazzy Vance and outfielder Ernie Orsatti. The Lip owed everybody in St. Louis money, and once told general manager Rickey that he'd win the

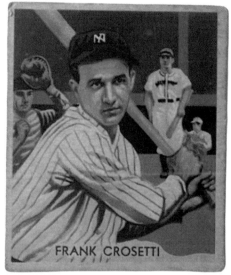

The Cardinals had their share of good baserunners in the 1940s, but Whitey Kurowski wasn't one of them. Kurowski got trapped in a rundown (left) in Game 6 of the 1944 World Series against the crosstown Browns, and was sandwiched by second baseman Don Gutteridge and first baseman George McQuinn. Kurowski was tagged out, but the Cards won the game, 3–1, to clinch the Series.

FRANK CROSETTI

Yankee shortstop Frank Crosetti would have fit in well with St. Louis' scrappy, aggressive style of play. Crosetti led the AL eight times in getting hit by pitched balls, and in 1938 he led the league with 27 steals.

pennant for him, but only if he received a raise. Vance, who had enjoyed success earlier in his career, but was now reaching the end of the line, was famous for a drink he had invented called the "Dazz-Marie." The ingredients were rye, bourbon, scotch, gin, sloe gin, vermouth, brandy and Benedictine, and they were poured into a large glass full of ice and then topped with powdered sugar. And the handsome Orsatti, who had a role in *Death on the Diamond,* a movie shot in Sportsman's Park during the season, was always inventing ingenious ways to stay out beyond curfew.

With such characters, the Cardinals' clubhouse sometimes came close to exploding. Medwick and Dizzy Dean were often at odds. On one occasion, the two were engaged in a shouting match in the dugout during a game. Dizzy and his brother Paul started toward Medwick, who picked up a bat and threatened to use it on them. Later in the game, Medwick slugged a grand slam. Back in the dugout, he spat a mouthful of water on Dizzy's shoes. "All right you big meathead," he snarled at the pitcher, "there's your three runs and one extra. Let's see you hold the damned lead."

The Cards had to overcome a big Giants' lead going into September. Only by going 21–7 that month to the Giants' 13–14 did St. Louis win the pennant and the chance to face the heavily favored Detroit Tigers, a team also known for its aggressiveness.

Dizzy Dean won the opener, 8–3. But he raised Frisch's blood pressure by arriving late to the park for the second game the next day, draping a tiger skin around his uniform and joining a marching band on the field.

Martin was himself, running the bases with abandon and diving headlong into Detroit players who happened to be in his way. One such collision injured Detroit's catcher-manager Cochrane, and Tiger baserunners retaliated by

Continued on page 158

Spikes

The material of choice has changed from kangaroo leather to cowhide or synthetic leather, and all players now have a pair of rubber-cleated shoes for artificial turf, but baseball spikes are largely the same now as they were in 1900: leather shoes with two sets of three metal spikes screwed, riveted or embedded into the soles. Spikes were standard equipment by the 1880s, when Cleveland Spiders manager Patsy Tebeau was among the first to have his players sharpen theirs to intimidate the opposition. The game stayed pretty rough into the early 1900s, and the use of spikes as a weapon caused some to call for their abolition. One writer suggested in 1909 that "a player whose spikes injured another player be forced to remain inactive as long as his victim." But the furor subsided, and the game became somewhat more genteel as the century wore on.

Metal spikes can injure the player wearing them almost as easily as they can one's opponent. Ankles and knees can be torn up when players change direction and their spikes catch in the turf or dirt. Hitters use them to dig trenches in the batter's box, and pitchers use them to scoop out a launching pad in front of the rubber, but spikes are most dear to the baserunner. They help him get a good jump when trying to steal, round the bases efficiently, and put the fear of God into infielders.

Babe Ruth—1920s

Ted Williams—1960

Nolan Ryan—1970s

19th Century

Mike Schmidt—1970s

Quickness and range in the field earned Cardinal shortstop Marty Marion the nickname "the Octopus." Marion (above, right, avoiding Brooklyn's Pete Reiser in 1942) led NL shortstops in fielding percentage four times, and in 1944 was named the NL's Most Valuable Player, despite hitting just .267.

repeatedly banging into Frisch at second base. Frisch and Durocher then responded by roughing up Detroit's leadoff hitter, Jo-Jo White, the next time he slid into second. Frisch sat on White's back; Durocher, on his head.

The Series umpires felt the heat of battle, too. Cardinal catcher DeLancey was fined after cursing at length for the benefit of umpire Brick Owens. Umpire Bill Klem and Detroit's Goose Goslin got into a heated argument in a hotel elevator. Fans were there to witness the exchange, and they were outraged; Commissioner Landis was forced to fine both Klem and Goslin in order to counteract the bad publicity.

St. Louis lost Game 4, 10–4, and almost lost Dean as well. In the fourth inning, with the Cardinals trailing, 4–3, Dean pinch-ran for Spud Davis. In trying to break up a double play, Dean was hit in the forehead and knocked out by the relay throw to first. After the game, Frisch tried to explain to the press why his star pitcher was pinch-running: "For one thing, we do have only a 21-man roster, and Spud is slow. For another, Dean is a helluva good athlete, and fast." Fortunately for Frisch, Dean was able to come back; he pitched the Cards to a Series victory in Game 7.

By 1942 none of the Gashouse Gang characters was wearing a Cardinal uniform. General manager Rickey, who would shortly move on to Brooklyn, had replaced the older, slower stars who commanded big salaries with newcomers who would play for less money—and who could run. He had no trouble finding such players in the St. Louis farm system, widely acknowledged to be the best in baseball.

The 1942 Cards, one of the best teams in baseball history, also became the youngest team to capture a pennant since the dead-ball era. The wartime

Cards relied on speed, defense and pitching. New York cartoonist Willard Mullin hung the nickname "St. Louis Swifties" on the team, and it stuck. Chicago Cubs manager Jimmie Wilson said of the club, "Too much energy, entirely too much. No team can keep charging around a park the way they do and stay in one piece. The Cardinals knock you out of the way just for fun."

Although they hit only 60 home runs, the Cards were always forcing the action on the bases, so much so that they led the league in runs scored. Typical was a play in a late-season game against the Cubs. Stan Musial, then a rookie, was on second when Coaker Triplett hit a slow dribbler in front of the plate. Chicago catcher Clyde McCullough went out for the ball, but his throw to first was too late to get Triplett. McCullough, who by then was away from the plate, and first baseman Babe Dahlgren argued the call, and Musial sped around third and scored.

Hailing from Donora, Pennsylvania, Musial was known as "the Donora Greyhound." Playing left field for the Cardinals, he constituted one-third of one of the speediest outfields in baseball. Center fielder Terry Moore—the oldest Cardinal at 30—reached everything hit his way, and right fielder Enos Slaughter was known for his hustle. Billy Herman, who played for Brooklyn that year, remembered one of the Cards' late-season visits to Ebbets Field. "I don't know how many extra-base hits they took away from us that day. We just couldn't believe what they were doing out there. It just got to the point where it didn't pay to belt one into the outfield." It didn't pay to hit it near shortstop Marty Marion or second baseman Frank "Creepy" Crespi, either.

Despite this talented cast, the Cardinals did not coast to the pennant; they put together a remarkable streak—winning 43 of their last 51 games—to edge Brooklyn by two games. The Dodgers, managed by ex-Gashouse Gang

Extra bases—not stolen bases—were Stan Musial's forte. Musial (above, scoring past Braves catcher Ernie Lombardi in 1942) led the NL eight times in doubles and five times in triples. According to Cardinal catcher Joe Garagiola, the best way to pitch to Musial was to "walk him and then try to pick him off first base."

member Leo Durocher, were perhaps even more aggressive than the Cards.
Still, St. Louis' style of play won admiration, and Brooklyn's, scorn. In August Casey Stengel, then the manager of the Boston Braves, blasted the
Dodgers after the lowly Braves won a game marred by an unprecedented
beanball war. Said Stengel: "If I had a ballclub as good as Durocher's, I
wouldn't throw at a ballclub as bad as mine. We're going to battle these guys
all the harder from now on, and I've talked to Frisch [at Pittsburgh] and Wilson, and other managers who feel the same. Sure they've got a big lead. But
they're not in yet. . . . Those jack-rabbits from St. Louis are coming." The
St. Louis jackrabbits did take the pennant, and went on to beat the heavily
favored, DiMaggio-led Yankees, four games to one, in the World Series.

It would be stretching the point to call the 1946 Cardinals "jack-rabbits,"
but speed did play a vital role in their strategy against the Boston Red Sox
in the World Series. In Game 7, center fielder Moore stopped a first-
inning Red Sox rally by racing from right center to left center to snatch a Ted
Williams drive. One of the most famous plays in World Series history occurred in the eighth inning of the same game. The score was tied, 3–3.
Slaughter, who had been injured in Game 5 but had refused to miss any action, led off the inning with a single to center. He then sat at first as Whitey
Kurowski popped out attempting a sacrifice bunt, and Del Rice flied deep to
Williams. With two outs, Slaughter was set to run with the pitch. Earlier in
the Series, while trying to score, Slaughter had been held up at third base by
coach Mike Gonzalez. Slaughter had been so enraged that manager Eddie
Dyer had finally said, "All right, all right, if it happens again and you think you
can score, go ahead. I'll take the rap."

Facing pitcher Bob Klinger, Harry Walker lined a hit to left center. Under normal circumstances, the fleet Dom DiMaggio would have been in center. But in the top of the eighth inning, DiMaggio had twisted his ankle running out a double. He had been replaced in the field by Leon Culberson. Culberson ran the ball down and threw it back to shortstop Johnny Pesky, who was standing in shallow left field. But Slaughter knew that Culberson had neither the speed nor the arm of DiMaggio, and he just kept running. Gonzalez started to put his hands up to stop Slaughter at third, but gave up when he saw the look on Slaughter's face.

Some witnesses say that Pesky hesitated before turning around and throwing the ball home. Pesky has always maintained that he did not. Whatever the case, the throw was up the line, and Slaughter scored. Walker took second and was credited with a double.

The Red Sox failed to score in the top of the ninth, and the Cardinals won the Series. It was their last World Series appearance until the arrival of Lou Brock and the resurgence of the running game 18 years later. ◗

Enos Slaughter's dash from first all the way home on Harry Walker's liner to left center has been hailed as one of the most daring runs in baseball history. It came in the eighth inning of Game 7 of the 1946 World Series against Boston and gave the Cardinals a 4–3 win.

Pepper Martin

Pepper Martin was not known for his hitting; he was inconsistent at the plate. Nor was he much of a fielder; as a third baseman he stopped more balls with his chest than with his glove. But his speed set him apart. One of the fastest men to play baseball in the 1930s, Martin led the National League in stolen bases three times.

It wasn't just sheer speed on the basepaths that made him great to watch; it was his breakneck style of play. An easygoing farm boy off the field, Martin was a die-hard competitor on the field. He ran the bases aggressively, sliding in on his stomach, knocking over whoever stood in his way. "When [Martin] ran," wrote sportswriter Red Smith, "he took flight wings beating, beak splitting the wind, and when he stole a base he swooped down on it with a predator's headlong dive." He played defense the same way: as a third baseman, Martin discouraged bunts by aiming his throws not at the first baseman but at the runner.

Martin signed with St. Louis in 1924, came up to the majors in 1928 and was ferried between the majors and minors for three seasons before becoming a Cardinal starter. In mid-1931 Cards general manager Branch Rickey put him in center field, replacing the more tested—and more expensive—veteran center fielder Taylor Douthit. St. Louis went on to take the NL pennant just as Martin was settling in at center. When the World Series began, few people, even in St. Louis, knew who Martin was. But by the time the Series was in full swing, the papers were billing it as "Pepper Martin vs. the Philadelphia Athletics."

In Game 1 Martin had three hits and a stolen base in a losing cause for St. Louis; in Game 2, he had two hits and two stolen bases and scored both runs in St. Louis' 2–0 win over Philadelphia. By this time, Martin's unbridled play had stolen the spotlight; one reporter revived the nickname Martin had earned for his high school football feats, "the Wild Hoss of the Osage"—a name that stuck well after the Series was over. And Martin was enough of a character to provide the sports pages with plenty of color commentary himself. When another reporter asked him where he had learned to run, Martin answered, "Well, sir, I grew up in Oklahoma and out there, once you start running there ain't nothing to stop you."

In Game 3 Martin singled and doubled, helping St. Louis to a 5–2 win. Philadelphia took Game 4 as George Earnshaw pitched a two-hitter; both hits were Martin's. In Game 5 Martin bunted safely once, then hit a home run with a man on in the sixth inning to lead the Cardinals to a 5–1 victory. In Games 6 and 7 Martin was hitless, but still got all the attention with two walks, a stolen base, and a running catch of a shallow blooper in the ninth inning of the final game to save the game and the Series for St. Louis.

Martin's performance was all the more remarkable considering the company he kept; as the Series standout, he stole the thunder from Al Simmons, Mickey Cochrane, Lefty Grove and Frankie Frisch. It was a rare collection of talented ballplayers: eight participants in the 1931 Cardinals-Athletics Series later made it to the Hall of Fame; Martin was not among them.

In 1932 Martin hit a slump. He stole just nine bases and hit a pitiful .238. But he rebounded in 1933, hitting .316 and leading the league with 26 steals and 122 runs scored. That pattern continued throughout his career. Though no one ever accused Martin of slacking off, he was dogged by inconsistency: he played like a sandlot bum one day and like a Hall of

Pepper Martin was usually all smiles, but after sitting on the Cardinal bench for the first part of the 1931 season, he issued a "play-me-or-trade-me" ultimatum to general manager Branch Rickey. Rickey played him, and St. Louis won a world title.

Famer the next. He was never consistent in any category save one: generating excitement.

Martin's intensity on the field coupled with his easygoing nature in the dugout made him the best-liked Cardinal on a team of characters that included Dizzy Dean, Joe Medwick and Leo Durocher. Martin rarely shaved and never bothered himself with details such as underwear or a protective cup, and most people believe that the Gashouse Gang got its scrappy image from his forever dirty—and sometimes torn—uniform. His style of play was infectious, and he was clearly the team's emotional leader. As manager Frisch said: "Put him on first base and you've got to call the cops to keep him off second. And the rest of the boys are the same way."

Martin didn't have a bad year in 1934: he hit .289 and led the league with 23 stolen bases. The Cardinals, however, had a great year: they won 95 games to edge the powerful New York Giants and take the NL flag, and they beat Detroit, four games to three, in a tightly contested World Series. Though he didn't dominate the Series as he had in 1931, Martin did have a good one—offensively. He was the hero of Game 3, hitting a double and a triple and scoring two of his teams four runs. He batted .355 over seven games, which gave him a lifetime Series average of .418—still the best ever among players with at least 50 World Series at-bats. But Martin set another record in that 1934 Series: his four errors at third base were the most of any player at that position in a seven-game series.

After he retired from the Cardinals in 1944, Martin became a minor league manager, exhibiting the same drive to win that he had as a player. On one occasion, while managing a game in Miami, he tried to choke an umpire. When he went before Commissioner Happy Chandler, who suggested to those present that Martin had meant no harm, Martin set the record straight. "I wanted to kill the buzzard," he said.

That was typical of Martin—an honest, easygoing man who became possessed the minute he set foot on a baseball diamond. Said Ripper Collins, Martin's teammate on the Cardinals, "That Martin is the kind of fellow who'd kill you with a slide just to get to the next base. If you survived, he'd stay up all night nursing you back to good health. Then, the next day, he'd be at you again!"

Martin scored five runs in the 1931 World Series against Philadelphia, but the one he scored in the seventh inning of Game 2 was a personal showcase. He singled, stole second (left), went to third on a ground out and scored past catcher Mickey Cochrane on a squeeze bunt (below). The Athletics' Al Simmons (right) had eight RBI in the Series, but Martin wielded the biggest bat, with four doubles and a home run among his 12 hits.

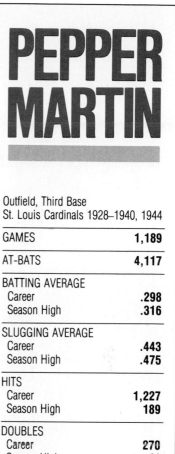

PEPPER MARTIN

Outfield, Third Base
St. Louis Cardinals 1928–1940, 1944

GAMES	**1,189**
AT-BATS	**4,117**
BATTING AVERAGE	
Career	**.298**
Season High	**.316**
SLUGGING AVERAGE	
Career	**.443**
Season High	**.475**
HITS	
Career	**1,227**
Season High	**189**
DOUBLES	
Career	**270**
Season High	**41**
TRIPLES	
Career	**75**
Season High	**12**
HOME RUNS	
Career	**59**
Season High	**11**
RUNS BATTED IN	
Career	**501**
Season High	**76**
RUNS	
Career	**756**
Season High	**122**
STOLEN BASES	
Career	**146**
Season High	**26**
STOLEN-BASE TITLES, NL	**1933, 1934, 1936**
WORLD SERIES	**1928, 1931, 1934**

Steal of the Century

"He moves like a man who knows Tae Kwon Do. Short and sudden. First of all quiet, then whomp! Like a cat pouncin'. Actually, like a panther. . . . He just sits back very still, looking like a statue. Then all of a sudden he leaps, and you sit there, wonderin' how anyone can move from zero velocity to the speed of light like that."

—Ernie Banks on Lou Brock

When more than 600 major league ballplayers, managers and coaches from every era of the 20th century were surveyed a few years ago, they overwhelmingly selected Lou Brock as the greatest base-stealer in history. Little wonder. Until Rickey Henderson broke it in 1991, Brock held the major league career record for steals with 938—46 more than Ty Cobb and one better than Sliding Billy Hamilton, a 19th century great whose total is inflated because it includes such things as advancing from first to third or second to home on a single. Besides the career mark, Brock holds the World Series mark with two seven-steal Series, and his single-season total of 118 in 1974 was a major league record until 1982, when it was broken by Henderson with 130. In addition, Brock led the National League in steals for eight of his 19 seasons, and he holds the record for most seasons stealing 50 or more bases by achieving the mark for 12 straight years.

Had those who voted Brock the best base-stealer been asked to select the trade that was the biggest steal of the last 30 years, they may well have named the June 15, 1964, trade that sent Brock from the Chicago Cubs to the St. Louis Cardinals in exchange for pitcher Ernie Broglio. Four other journeymen players were involved, but for all practical purposes, the trade was Brock for Broglio.

At the time, it looked like a great deal for the Cubs. "Thank you, thank you, oh, you lovely St. Louis Cardinals. Nice doing business with you. Please call again any time." So wrote Bob Smith, a sports reporter for the *Chicago Daily News*. And with some justification. The 24-year-old Brock had, in two and a half years as a Cubs' outfielder, failed to distinguish himself. He was hitting a mediocre .251 at the time of the deal. The 28-year-old Broglio, on

Boston's Jim Lonborg won battles with St. Louis' Lou Brock in Games 2 and 5 of the 1967 World Series, holding the Cardinal leadoff man hitless in eight at-bats. But Brock won the war with two hits and three stolen bases in Game 7 (preceding page), and the Cards won the Series, 7–2.

the other hand, had been a 20-game winner in 1960 and had won 18 games and posted a 2.99 ERA in the year prior to the trade.

Many of the Cardinals agreed with the *Daily News'* Smith. National League President Bill White, then a St. Louis first baseman, recalled, "We thought we had given up too much. Brock was not a good fielder, he struck out a lot, didn't know how to run the bases." Although Brock had stolen a respectable 50 bases in his short career, he had been caught stealing 22 times; his poor success ratio hardly justified the effort. Still, it was rare to find anyone in a Cubs uniform running at all, and when the trade was made, *Chicago Tribune* sportswriter Richard Dozer observed, "But possessed of tremendous speed, Brock could prove to be a sound investment for the Cardinals."

A sound investment indeed. Sent to the plate as a pinch hitter, Brock struck out on three pitches in his first at-bat as a Cardinal. But the next night, in his first start, he had three hits, two stolen bases and scored both runs in a 2–1 St. Louis victory over Houston. He was off and running, and so was his new team. Brock batted .348 and stole 33 bases in 103 games, as the Cards—who were 21–28 at the time of the trade—went on to steal the National League pennant from Philadelphia. The Cards finished 93–69. Meanwhile, the Cubs—who were 27–27 when the deal was struck—finished the season at 76–86, good enough for eighth place in the ten-team league. Broglio, troubled by a sore arm, went 4–7 for Chicago.

Career comparisons between Brock and Broglio were even more disastrous for the Cubs' faithful. Broglio's physical ills continued, and he re-

The Cubs' power-oriented style of play during the early 1960s had a chilling effect on Brock's talent. It wasn't until he was traded to St. Louis in 1964 that he started playing well in Chicago's Wrigley Field. "He loved to beat us, and he made an extra-special effort to do so," said Cub first baseman Ernie Banks. "The Bleacher Bums in Wrigley Field knew that, so they gave him an extra-special kind of hell."

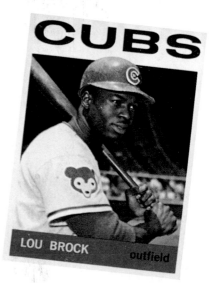

CUBS

LOU BROCK outfield

Brock (above, beating the tag of Philadelphia's Mike Schmidt) might have stolen even more bases if his extra-base power didn't land him on second or third so often. From 1963 to 1969, Brock averaged 31 doubles, 11 triples and 13 home runs a season.

tired after the 1966 season, having gone 7–19 in his two and a half years with Chicago. Brock banged out 3,023 hits over his 19-year career and hit over .300 eight times to go along with his base-stealing feats.

And the teams? The Cubs never made it to postseason play during the years that Brock remained active. The Cardinals, who had not won a pennant since 1946, won three league titles with Brock, and thanks in part to clutch performances by the outfielder, they were triumphant in two World Series.

Whether the Cubs would have achieved such success had Brock remained in Chicago is, of course, speculative, although the 1969 Cubs, who were overtaken by the Mets at the end of the season, could certainly have used him. It is doubtful whether Brock himself would have achieved such success had he stayed at Wrigley Field, which encourages players to hit home runs rather than play a speed-based game, instead of moving to Busch Stadium, where speed is king.

Statisticians such as John Thorn and Pete Palmer argue that Brock wasn't such a bargain after all. They point out that Brock didn't walk enough for a leadoff man and that he had a relatively low on-base percentage of .344. They say, too, that he struck out too much—1,730 times—and was a poor outfielder. They even dismiss his stolen-base records.

Statisticians notwithstanding, Brock was successful in over 75 percent of his attempts and set the all-time record, playing 657 fewer games than Ty Cobb. And he impressed those in the press box as well as those in the cheap seats. Brock was elected by the Baseball Writers Association of America to the Hall of Fame in 1985, the first year he was eligible.

That Lou Brock ever made it to the major leagues, much less Cooperstown, was quite an achievement. He was born in El Dorado, Arkansas, in

1939, the seventh child of Mrs. Paralee Brock, a single parent who worked as a field hand and domestic worker to support her family. He grew up in Collinston, Louisiana, a town of 300, and despite hitting .540 his senior year in high school and finishing third in his graduating class of 105, he did not receive any athletic scholarship offers from colleges. Nor did he elicit a single query from a baseball scout.

Undaunted, Brock earned a spot as a walk-on at Southern University in Baton Rouge, and went on to bat .545 the next season and lead his team to an NAIA championship. A solid 5′ 11½″, 170 pounds, he earned high marks for speed *and* power, hitting 13 home runs in 27 games. His speed apparently impressed others more than it did Brock. In his autobiography, *Stealing Is My Game,* Brock acknowledges that he was always fast, but adds, "All the kids in Collinston were fast."

By 1960 the Cubs had seen enough of this particular kid from Collinston to offer him a contract. And by 1962 he was the team's starting center fielder. He batted .263 and stole 16 bases. Meanwhile, on the West Coast, the Dodgers' Maury Wills was shattering Cobb's long-standing single-season stolen-base mark.

Brock's major accomplishment during his rookie season was not achieved on the basepaths, but at the plate. He hit a booming home run over the center field wall in the old Polo Grounds, where the Mets played before moving to Shea Stadium. The wall stood 483 feet from home plate, and Brock became only the third player ever to put the ball over it. Coincidentally, perhaps, the very next day, the decision was made to tear down the Polo Grounds.

Brock always seemed to save his best—and most powerful—work for the World Series. His homer off Detroit's Pat Dobson (above) in Game 1 in 1968 was one of four Brock hit in three World Series. His .391 Series average and .655 slugging percentage rank second and fifth, respectively, on the all-time list.

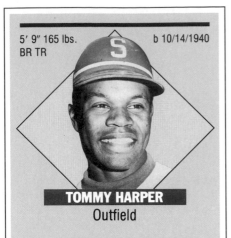

TOMMY HARPER
Outfield

5' 9" 165 lbs.
BR TR
b 10/14/1940

In 1961, his first full year in the minors, Tommy Harper knocked 'em dead. With Topeka, he hit over .320, led the Triple I League in walks and runs, and was voted league MVP.

But Harper's consistency went awry in the majors, aggravated by frequent moves—he played for eight teams in 15 years—and shuffling of his position, from outfield to infield and back again. His batting average never made it to the .300 mark, but fans loved watching the little guy rattle a pitcher with his speed on the basepaths, and he stole at least 25 bases nine times.

Harper started in the majors with Cincinnati in 1962 and had a solid year for the Reds in 1965. In 159 games, he hit .257 with 35 stolen bases and led the league in runs scored with 126. In 1966 he got his batting average up to .278, but a fractured wrist put him on the bench in 1967. In November he was traded to Cleveland, where he had a disappointing year.

But in the fall of 1968, Harper was drafted by the Seattle Pilots and he revived for the expansion team. He racked up a league-leading 73 stolen bases—the most in the league since Ty Cobb's 96 in 1915. In 1970 Harper slugged 31 homers and stole 38 bases to become one of the few players in history to hit more than 30 home runs and steal 30 bases in the same season.

Harper retired after the 1976 season with a career total of 408 stolen bases—26th on the all-time list.

St. Louis center fielder Bake McBride (above, sliding) hit .309 and stole 30 bases as a rookie in 1974, but hardly anyone noticed, because the guy who played left field—Lou Brock—stole 118. Undaunted, McBride hit .300 and stole 26 the following year.

Brock batted .258 and stole 24 bases in 36 attempts his second year, but despite his speed, he was deemed a liability in the field. The *Daily News'* Smith wrote, "If you have watched all the Cub home games thus far, you probably have come to the conclusion that Lou Brock is the worst outfielder in baseball history. He really isn't, but he hasn't done much to prove [otherwise]."

Years later, Brock admitted that he had had his problems as a fielder at Wrigley, but he recalled one catch that he did make on a Vada Pinson drive which helped to turn his career around. When he was signed by the Cubs, Brock gave himself three years to make it in professional baseball; he vowed that if he didn't consider himself a success after that time, he would quit. When Pinson, the Cincinnati Reds' fine hitting outfielder, came to the plate at Wrigley in May 1964, Brock was already past his self-imposed deadline. Pinson hit a screaming line drive to right center field. Brock assumed it would be a high, off-the-wall double. He raced for the ball and leaped, as he describes it, not to catch the ball, but to show that he had tried. Remarkably, he did catch the ball, though he didn't know it for several moments. After hitting the wall, he searched desperately for the ball on the ground around him, panicking, before he thought to look in his glove. The catch, he says, persuaded him that he could make it. "I am good enough. I can do it. I'm staying," he remembers thinking. But he wasn't staying in Chicago. Less than a month later, he was traded.

Why the speedy turnaround from mediocrity to excellence when he reached St. Louis? Brock attributed the change to a number of factors. The atmosphere in St. Louis, for one. The Cubs' locker room had been solemn;

the Cards' clubhouse was loose, more fun. The Cards were also managed differently than the Cubs were, and during Brock's rookie year, the Cubs had not been managed at all, but had been run by owner Philip Wrigley's ill-fated "College of Coaches" system. A different Cubs coach took over every few weeks, leading to chronic confusion and lack of direction. But St. Louis was guided by one man, manager Johnny Keane. Brock immediately noticed that Keane operated his club on the principle of individual independence. "If you wanted to do something, you did it; you didn't have to fill out forms," Brock remembers.

"Once—this was a major turning point in my experience, I recall—Keane said to me, 'Since you've got the speed for it, I guess you're going to want to try stealing bases.'

" 'Hell yes, sure,' I said.

" 'Well, you're on. Go when it seems right to go.' That's all he said.

"My impulse was to ask him when that was supposed to be, Mr. Keane? Under what conditions? Who gives me the sign? Are there different instructions for right- and left-handed pitchers? But I restrained myself. It was clear he was telling me that the decision was essentially mine to make. Wow. I had to keep rubbing my eyes."

Such a system was unheard of in Chicago, and Brock concluded that the teams simply had different philosophies. The Cards encouraged players to play their strengths, while the Cubs asked their men to concentrate on their failings in order to correct them. The Chicago system's effect on Brock was stifling. It turned him into, in his words, "an overthink machine" who, while trying to correct weaknesses, became less steady at the things he excelled in, such as running.

Lou Brock led the NL in steals every year from 1966 to 1974, except in 1970, when Cincinnati's Bobby Tolan (above) beat him out, 57–51. Two years later Tolan stole 42 bases, and added five more in the World Series against Oakland.

The Best on the Bases

The more often you get on base, the more chances you have to steal, so the list of all-time great base-stealers includes some fine batting averages and on-base percentages. And though base-stealers may differ in size and style, they have one thing in common — daring. They all get caught, but as Maury Wills said, getting caught is "like getting thrown off a horse; you have to get right back on." Below are the career numbers of 13 of the greatest base-stealers in history. Caught-stealing statistics were not kept consistently until 1928 in the AL, 1951 in the NL.

Name	Years played	H	R	BA	On-base %	Stolen bases	Stolen base %
Honus Wagner	1897-1917	3,430	1,740	.329	.386	722	—
Ty Cobb	1905-1928	4,191	2,245	.367	.429	892	—
Eddie Collins	1906-1930	3,311	1,818	.333	.420	743	—
Max Carey	1910-1929	2,665	1,545	.285	.356	738	—
Luis Aparicio	1956-1973	2,677	1,335	.262	.311	506	.788
Maury Wills	1959-1972	2,134	1,067	.281	.330	586	.738
Lou Brock	1961-1979	3,023	1,610	.293	.341	938	.753
Bert Campaneris	1964-1983	2,249	1,181	.259	.308	649	.765
Joe Morgan	1963-1984	2,518	1,651	.271	.393	689	.810
Davey Lopes	1972-1987	1,671	1,023	.263	.348	557	.830
Willie Wilson*	1976-	2,038	1,098	.287	.323	632	.836
Rickey Henderson*	1979-	1,888	1,395	.291	.401	994	.813
Vince Coleman*	1985-	1,008	611	.264	.327	586	.820

* Statistics are current through the 1991 season.

Brock's remarks about getting the green light to steal reveal the fragile psyche of the professional ballplayer. He says: "Even if the coaches [in Chicago] had said to me, 'Steal when you want to,' I don't think I would have done it. If you decide to bolt for second base, and when you're halfway there it suddenly seems a bad idea, you're not about to turn around and go back. On the other hand, the prospect of getting shot down and going back to the dugout to hear about it is not attractive either.

"So you spend your time at first base thinking about all this, which does nothing but give you ulcers, divert your attention from home plate and use up precious time. The simplest solution is just not to make a run for it." The image of Lou Brock frozen in fear at first base is today hard to conjure.

There was a final difference between the two clubs—this one on the field. Says Brock, "The Cardinals were a scrambling team. They were built for speed and daring. They played for one run at a time, not like the Cubs, who were geared for the big inning." Given carte blanche by Keane, Brock, in effect, kept charging for the next 15 years, breaking the records of both Wills and Cobb along the way. Inevitably, the three are often compared, not just statistically, but stylistically and, for that matter, personally.

Despite the fact that every great base-stealer says that sheer speed is no guarantee of success on the basepaths, fans are always curious to know who is the fastest. Since none of the three ever raced one another, it is impossible to crown a speed king. But most observers who saw both Wills and Brock say that Brock was faster. As evidence, they note that Brock, able to rely on his speed more than Wills, took a much more conservative lead off the base than did the Dodger great, who was famous for being so far off first—up to five and a half steps—that he almost always had to dive back to the base.

Wills wore the infield dirt as a badge of courage. Brock, on the other hand, rarely ventured more than three and a half to four steps off the bag, explaining, "For comfort everyone decides on his own maximum point. I seldom go out so far that I have to come back to the base head-first."

Cardinals catcher Tim McCarver said of Brock: "He is a more intimidating base-stealer than Wills was. Wills didn't have Brock's speed. Maury probably stretched his ability as much as he could. That's not saying Lou hasn't stretched his ability, too. It's just that Lou has that much more to work with."

Wills, however, is not convinced that Brock was faster. In his autobiography, Wills recalls that he frequently challenged Brock to a race. " 'Let's go, Lou,' I'd say as we talked before a game. 'Let's have it out. One race to end all. You and me.'

" 'You don't mean that, Maury,' Lou would say. 'You really want to race me?'

" 'Anytime,' I'd say.'

"Then he'd laugh and I'd laugh, and somehow the years passed and we never did race. I wish we had."

Former Cubs first baseman Ernie Banks says Brock would have won the race, but adds that while Brock may have been faster and the two took different leads and slides—Wills had a broad hook, while Brock's slide was much shorter—they were similar in one important respect. "It's their brains," Banks says. "I've seen Lou—and Maury—both psych out a pitcher as if they were inside the man's head, just readin' the meter."

Cobb, too, was a student of the game, and had he possessed the technology in the early days of the century, perhaps he would have gone to the

Tommie Agee—whether playing with the AL's White Sox or the NL's Mets—resembled Brock. He was fast and powerful and struck out too much. Agee (above, tumbling past Phillies shortstop Larry Bowa) averaged 26 steals, 18 homers and 123 strikeouts a season from 1966 to 1971.

Brock was a master at reading pitchers' movements, probably because he spent more time watching them than any other base-stealer. "Arrogance is important," he said, "but you can't have it until you have knowledge. And you only get knowledge by intensive study."

extreme of filming opposing pitchers as Brock did. Brock usually brought his camera to spring training and filmed pitchers from the safety of the Cardinals' dugout. But once, he brazenly stationed himself with a movie camera along the foul line to capture the moves of Dodger great Don Drysdale. Drysdale eventually chased him from the field, but it was too late. "I had him and his motion stuck on a frame so I could study it—and there was not a thing he was able to do about it," Brock later said.

Brock also used a stopwatch to time pitchers' moves and catchers' throws, and he was always aware of his own time on the basepaths. When he broke Wills' single-season record in 1974, he was already 35 years old and, he told reporters, two steps slower than he had been in his prime. "I used to get down to first base in 3.4 or 3.5, but now it's 3.9 or 4.0 flat. My very best effort now is 3.8. That in itself shows I'm three to five feet slower."

By that time in his career, Brock's quick mind made up for his slower feet. It allowed him to outsmart the Phillies' great defensive catcher, Bob Boone, for one. Coming into the September 10, 1977, game between Philadelphia and St. Louis, Boone had thrown out 20 consecutive runners. When Brock reached first, he imitated the infielder's cry, "There he goes!" Boone came up throwing, but Brock had not moved. On the next pitch, Brock played the same game with the same result. Not wanting to be embarrassed a third time, Boone clutched the ball on the next pitch, as a silent Brock stole second.

While such antics call to mind Cobb, who was famous for yelling at pitchers and catchers, Brock was usually a much quieter presence than his predecessor. His teammates and opponents held him in high esteem, unlike Cobb,

In 1985 Vince Coleman renewed the St. Louis tradition of having the best base-stealer in the NL playing left field. Coleman stole at least 100 bases in each of his first three seasons, an unprecedented feat.

Brock had outstanding physical skills, but many claim it was his intelligence that made him great. "I suppose everyone agrees that what finally mattered most of all was that understanding of his," said Stan Musial, "that exceptional knowledge of the game in general and baserunning in particular that he had worked so hard to achieve over the years."

who was almost universally disliked because of his temper and arrogance. Still, on the field Brock possessed what he described as "a certain arrogance." He added: "I learned that you could have no fear of failure if you were fated to steal a lot of bases.... You're always on the verge of disaster as a basestealer. If you're thrown out you could be wiping out a big rally.

"Despite these thoughts you've got to have utter confidence in what you're doing and realize that it helps your team win games. You'll steal a base four or five times if you're good enough... and if they catch you, well, they owe you four."

In 1982 Brock watched as his single-season record of 118 steals was smashed by Rickey Henderson, who stole 130. And on May 1, 1991, he watched as Henderson stole his 939th base, eclipsing Brock's career mark. But Brock's description of Henderson betrays no jealousy, only respect: "Nobody his age has been good enough... and eliminated the word 'fear' like Rickey has. He has a baserunner's arrogance that is hard to get. And he has a burning desire for that moment when he is one step ahead of the tornado. He wants to become the tornado." Such words could be spoken only by a man who has been a step ahead of the storm himself. ◆

Lou Brock

The spitball that launched one of the greatest base-stealing careers of all time wasn't thrown in a ballpark. It was thrown in a school classroom in Collinston, Louisiana, missed its target and wound up hitting the teacher. The offending student was Lou Brock, and his punishment was to give an oral report on five of the great baseball players of the time—Roy Campanella, Joe DiMaggio, Stan Musial, Don Newcombe and Jackie Robinson.

The report spurred Brock's interest in baseball, especially when he found out that major league players received $8 a day in meal money. "All I could think of was how much penny candy that would buy." In high school, Brock became good at baseball, but he was better at math and won a partial academic scholarship to Southern University. He tried out for the baseball team as a freshman but was relegated to shagging flies until he collapsed in the outfield one day from heat exhaustion. "I came to and rested a little, and as a goodwill gesture, the coach let me hit," Brock said. "I took five swings and hit four balls out of the park."

Brock played on the U.S. team in the 1959 Pan-American Games—along with future major league stars Rico Carty and Juan Marichal—then dropped out of college after his junior year to sign with the Cubs. As a rookie with the Cubs in 1962, Brock honed his raw speed with help from a couple of former track stars—Iowa's Charles "Deacon" Jones and a guy named Jesse Owens, who had won four gold medals in the 1936 Summer Olympics.

After two and a half lackluster seasons with the Cubs, Brock was traded to the St. Louis Cardinals, where manager Johnny Keane turned him loose on the basepaths—and on the league. Brock rewarded Keane's faith by hitting .348 and helping the Cardinals win their first pennant since 1946. Brock then jacked his act up a notch in the 1964 World Series. In Game 1 against the Yankees, Brock singled in the first, went to third on a single and scored the game's first run on a sacrifice fly. In the second he threw a runner out at the plate from left field, and in the eighth he broke open a close game with a two-out, two-run double. He had three hits in Game 6, and homered in the Cards' 7-5 win in Game 7. But Brock's nine hits, five RBI and .300 average proved to be his poorest World Series performance.

St. Louis won another pennant in 1967, thanks in part to Brock's league-leading 113 runs scored, 52 stolen bases, 21 homers and .299 average. He became the first player in history to hit at least 20 homers and steal at least 50 bases in a season, and again, he got out of the gate early in the Series. He went 4 for 4 in Game 1, stole two bases and scored the Cardinals' only runs in a 2-1 win. In Game 3 he harassed a run out of Boston reliever Lee Stange: Brock beat out a bunt in the sixth, went to third on a wild pickoff throw by Stange and scored on a single by Roger Maris. And by the time Bob Gibson fanned Boston's George Scott to end Game 7, Brock had 12 hits, a record seven stolen bases, eight runs scored and a monstrous .414 average.

In 1968 Brock went himself one better with 13 hits, another seven steals, two homers, a .464 batting average and an .857 slugging percentage. But this time Gibson and the Cards wound up on the short end in Game 7.

While most base-stealers' totals flagged as their careers wore on and their legs wore down, Brock's increased. He brought a mathematician's precision

Lou Brock (above) was the master of the pop-up slide, which got him back up quickly and wasn't too hard on his legs. Brock was as successful in business as he was on the bases, and his "BroccaBrella" (left) was just one of his business interests.

Brock was a base-stealing scientist, but also found a role for art. "You've got to have a passion for the art," he said. "It's a love affair. When you're in love with something, you have no fear. You combine that with arrogance, and you can beat a pitcher every time."

and a student's incessant curiosity to all aspects of the running game, and in 1974, at the age of 35, shocked the baseball world with 118 steals. Brock's total shattered Maury Wills' record of 104, set in 1962, and proved that he stole as much with his smarts as his speed. He kept himself in outstanding physical condition, maximized every possible advantage a baserunner has, and was a master at the mind game between runner and pitcher. Brock explained his advantages to biographer Frank Schulze this way: "In the first place, once I'm on first base, I can take a modest lead and stand perfectly still, without giving away any significant information about myself. But the pitcher is obliged to move, just to deliver the pitch, and in moving he telegraphs a whole catalog of data about himself. Furthermore, he has two things on his mind: the batter *and* me. I have only one thing in mind—to steal off him. The very business of disconcerting him is marvelously complex." While Brock may have taken a more cerebral approach to base-stealing than many of the other all-time greats, that doesn't mean he wasn't as daring and arrogant as the rest. "Show me a guy who's afraid to look bad and I'll show you a guy you can beat every time," he said.

Off the field, however, Brock was a pussycat. And a slow one at that. "It's my personality," he said. "I dress slow. I walk slow. I even sit slow. When I get on the field I'm fast. But living and playing ball are two different things." A high-average leadoff hitter, Brock was criticized for striking out too much and for being a below-average outfielder. But he took it all in stride and remained remarkably consistent throughout his career, both on and off the field. He capitalized on his fame to become a successful businessman, and was so committed to working with youths in St. Louis that a boys' club was named after him. "Lou is one of the nicest, finest men ever to play this game," said Cardinal teammate Ted Simmons.

And while base-stealing won him fame, Brock always considered hitting his first priority. "Stealing is an option," he said. "Hitting is a necessity." In 1968 he became the first player since Honus Wagner in 1908 to lead the league in doubles, triples and stolen bases. "He's the greatest single offensive force I've seen," said Cardinal pitcher John Curtis. And in 1979, at the age of 40, he ended his career with a bang, hitting .304 with 21 stolen bases.

Unlike a lot of the great base-stealers of his time, Brock was as dangerous with his bat as he was on the basepaths. He provided a prototype for offensive firepower that has been duplicated by players like Joe Morgan, Cesar Cedeno and Rickey Henderson. And he provided the creed for this new breed of base-stealer when he said, "I don't have to steal bases, you see, to play," he said. "I steal because I want to."

LOU BROCK

Outfield
Chicago Cubs 1961–1964
St. Louis Cardinals 1964–1979
Hall of Fame 1985

GAMES	**2,616**
AT-BATS *(9th all time)*	**10,332**
BATTING AVERAGE	
Career	**.293**
Season High	**.315**
SLUGGING AVERAGE	
Career	**.410**
Season High	**.472**
HITS	
Career	**3,023**
Season High	**206**
DOUBLES	
Career	**486**
Season High	**46**
TRIPLES	
Career	**141**
Season High	**14**
HOME RUNS	
Career	**149**
Season High	**21**
RUNS BATTED IN	
Career	**900**
Season High	**76**
RUNS	
Career	**1,610**
Season High	**126**
STOLEN BASES	
Career *(2nd all time)*	**938**
Season High *(2nd all time)*	**118**
STOLEN-BASE TITLES, NL	
1966–1969, 1971–1974	
WORLD SERIES	**1964, 1967, 1968**

Lenny Dykstra isn't used to being thrown out, but when he is his reaction is predictably theatrical. Dykstra, here being tagged out by Pittsburgh third baseman Bobby Bonilla, stole 103 bases in his first four years with the Mets, with a success rate of 81 percent.

MOST STOLEN BASES

Career

1.	Rickey Henderson	994	1979-1991*
2.	Lou Brock	938	1961-1979
3.	Ty Cobb	892	1905-1928
4.	Eddie Collins	743	1906-1930
5.	Max Carey	738	1910-1929
6.	Honus Wagner	703	1897-1917
7.	Joe Morgan	689	1963-1984
8.	Tim Raines	679	1979-1991*
9.	Bert Campaneris	649	1964-1981, 1983
10.	Willie Wilson	632	1976-1991*
11.	Vince Coleman	586	1985-1991*
	Maury Wills	586	1959-1972
13.	Davey Lopes	557	1972-1987
14.	Cesar Cedeno	550	1970-1986
15.	Luis Aparicio	506	1956-1973
16.	Ozzie Smith	499	1978-1991*
17.	Clyde Milan	495	1907-1922
18.	Omar Moreno	487	1975-1986'
19.	Jimmy Sheckard	465	1897-1913
20.	Bobby Bonds	461	1968-1981
21.	Ron LeFlore	455	1974-1982
22.	Sherry Magee	441	1904-1919
23.	Tris Speaker	433	1907-1928
24.	Bob Bescher	428	1908-1918
25.	Frankie Frisch	419	1919-1937

* Active player

Season

1.	Rickey Henderson	130	1982
2.	Lou Brock	118	1974
3.	Vince Coleman	110	1985
4.	Vince Coleman	109	1987
5.	Rickey Henderson	108	1983
6.	Vince Coleman	107	1986
7.	Maury Wills	104	1962
8.	Rickey Henderson	100	1980
9.	Ron LeFlore	97	1980
10.	Ty Cobb	96	1915
	Omar Moreno	96	1980
12.	Maury Wills	94	1965
13.	Rickey Henderson	93	1988
14.	Tim Raines	90	1983
15.	Clyde Milan	88	1912
16.	Rickey Henderson	87	1986
17.	Ty Cobb	83	1911
	Willie Wilson	83	1979
19.	Eddie Collins	81	1910
	Bob Bescher	81	1911
	Vince Coleman	81	1988
22.	Rickey Henderson	80	1985
	Eric Davis	80	1986
24.	Dave Collins	79	1980
	Willie Wilson	79	1980

Rookie Season

1.	Vince Coleman	110	1985
2.	Benny Kauff	75	1914†
3.	Juan Samuel	72	1984
4.	Tim Raines	71	1981
5.	Hap Myers	57	1913
6.	Gene Richards	56	1977
7.	Emmet Heidrick	55	1899
8.	Bob Bescher	54	1909
9.	Donie Bush	53	1909
	Omar Moreno	53	1977
11.	Larry Lintz	50	1974
	John Cangelosi	50	1986
13.	Rollie Zeider	49	1910
	Sonny Jackson	49	1966
	Steve Sax	49	1982
16.	Gary Pettis	48	1984
17.	Willie Wilson	46	1978
18.	Jimmy Barrett	44	1900
	Tommie Agee	44	1966
20.	Josh DeVore	43	1910
	George Grantham	43	1923
22.	Roy Thomas	42	1899
	Mitchell Page	42	1977
	Bob Dernier	42	1982
	Delino DeShields	42	1990
26.	Bert Daniels	41	1910
	Joe Jackson	41	1911
	Milt Cuyler	41	1991

† Federal League

Most Steals in a Game

7	George Gore	6/25/1881‡
	Billy Hamilton	8/31/1884 (2nd game)‡
6	Eddie Collins	9/11/1912 and 9/22/1912 (1st game)
5	Dennis McGann	5/27/1904
	Clyde Milan	6/14/1912
	Johnny Neun	7/9/1927
	Amos Otis	9/7/1971
	Davey Lopes	8/24/1974
	Bert Campaneris	4/24/1976
	Lonnie Smith	9/4/1982
	Alan Wiggins	5/17/1984
	Tony Gwynn	9/20/1986

‡ Stolen bases not officially compiled until 1886

Eric Davis

MOST STEALS OF HOME

Career

1.	Ty Cobb	50	1905–1928
2.	Max Carey	33	1910–1929
3.	George Burns	28	1911–1925
4.	Honus Wagner	27	1897–1917
5.	Wildfire Schulte	23	1904–1918
	Sherry Magee	23	1904–1919
7.	Johnny Evers	21	1902–1929
8.	George Sisler	20	1915–1930
9.	Frankie Frisch	19	1919–1937
	Jackie Robinson	19	1947–1956
11.	Joe Tinker	18	1902–1916
	Tris Speaker	18	1907–1928
	Jimmy Sheckard	18	1897–1913
	Larry Doyle	17	1907–1920
	Eddie Collins	17	1906–1930
14.	Rod Carew	17	1967–1985
17.	Lou Gehrig	15	1923–1939
	Ben Chapman	15	1930–1946
19.	Fred Merkle	14	1907–1926
	Vic Saier	14	1911–1919
	Fritz Maisel	14	1913–1918

Season

7	Pete Reiser		1946
	Rod Carew		1969

MOST TRIPLES

Career

1.	Sam Crawford	312	1899–1917
2.	Ty Cobb	297	1905–1928
3.	Honus Wagner	252	1897–1917
4.	Jake Beckley	244	1888–1907
5.	Roger Connor	233	1880–1897
6.	Fred Clarke	223	1894–1915
	Tris Speaker	223	1907–1928
8.	Dan Brouthers	206	1879–1896, 1904
9.	Joe Kelley	194	1891–1906, 1908
10.	Paul Waner	190	1926–1945
11.	Bid McPhee	189	1882–1889
12.	Eddie Collins	187	1906–1930
13.	Harry Stovey	185	1880–1893
	Jesse Burkett	185	1890–1905
15.	Sam Rice	184	1915–1934
16.	Ed Delahanty	183	1888–1903
17.	Edd Roush	182	1913–1929, 1931
18.	Ed Konetchy	181	1907–1921
19.	Buck Ewing	178	1880–1897
20.	Rabbit Maranville	177	1912–1933, 1935
	Stan Musial	177	1941–1944, 1946–1963

Season

1.	Owen Wilson	36	1912
2.	Dave Orr	31	1886
	Heinie Reitz	31	1894
4.	Perry Werden	29	1893
5.	Harry Davis	28	1897
6.	George Davis	27	1893
	Sam Thompson	27	1894
	Jimmy Williams	27	1899
9.	Long John Reilly	26	1890
	George Treadway	26	1894
	Joe Jackson	26	1912
	Sam Crawford	26	1914
	Kiki Cuyler	26	1925

MOST INSIDE-THE-PARK HOME RUNS

Career

1.	Sam Crawford	50	1899–1917
2.	Tommy Leach	48	1898–1915, 1918
3.	Ty Cobb	47	1905–1928
4.	Honus Wagner	45	1897–1917
5.	Tris Speaker	36	1907–1928
6.	Jake Daubert	32	1910–1924
7.	Owen Wilson	31	1908–1916
8.	Rogers Hornsby	30	1915–1937
9.	Edd Roush	29	1913–1929, 1931
10.	Max Carey	28	1910–1929

FOR FURTHER READING

Charles C. Alexander, *Ty Cobb,* Oxford
  University Press, 1984.

Lou Brock, with Franz Schulze, *Stealing
  Is My Game,* Prentice Hall, 1976.

Steve Fiffer, *How to Watch Baseball,*
  Facts on File, 1987.

Whitey Herzog and Kevin Horrigan,
  White Rat, Harper & Row, 1987.

John B. Holway, *Blackball Stars,*
  Meckler Books, 1988.

Eric Nadel and Craig R. Wright, *The
  Man Who Stole First Base,* Taylor
  Publishing Co., 1989.

Maury Wills, with Don Freeman, *How
  to Steal a Pennant,* G. P. Putnam,
  1976.

PICTURE CREDITS

Front cover: Rickey Henderson by Ronald C. Modra/*Sports Illustrated*

Back cover: Ty Cobb National Baseball Library, Cooperstown, NY

Pages 4-5: Spectra-Action

The Artful Dodger
6 (all) Focus on Sports, Inc.; 7 AP/Wide World Photos; 8 Robert Riger; 9 (left) Fred Kaplan; 9 (right) National Baseball Library, Cooperstown, NY; 10 Jonathan Kronstadt Collection; 11 Malcolm W. Emmons; 13 Malcolm W. Emmons; 14 UPI/Bettmann Newsphotos; 15 Walter Iooss, Jr./*Sports Illustrated;* 16 Ron Menchine Collection/Renée Comet Photography; 17 Neil Leifer; *Sports Illustrated;* 18 (left) Walter Iooss, Jr./*Sports Illustrated;* 18 (right) Marvin E. Newman; 19 (top) Walter Iooss, Jr./*Sports Illustrated;* 19 (bottom) Richard Darcey.

Speedsters
20 Ron Vesely; 21 Brian Lanker/*Sports Illustrated;* 22 Walter Iooss, Jr.; 23 (left) Anthony Neste; 23 (right) Ron Menchine Collection/Renée Comet Photography; 24 (left) National Baseball Library, Cooperstown, NY; 24 (right) Carnegie Library of Pittsburgh; 25 Lewis Portnoy/Spectra-Action; 26 AP/Wide World Photos; 27 Marc S. Levine/Sportschrome East/West; 28 Thomas Carwile Collection/Renée Comet Photography; 29 National Baseball Library, Cooperstown, NY; 30 Ron Menchine Collection/Renée Comet Photography; 31 UPI/Bettmann Newsphotos; 32 Nancy Hogue; 33 Ron Vesely; 34-35 Mickey Pfleger; 36 (left) National Baseball Library, Cooperstown, NY; 36 (right) Louis A. Raynor/Sportschrome East/West; 37 Historical Society of Pennsylvania; 38 Lewis Portnoy/Spectra-Action; 39 Anthony Neste; 40 WOB Collection; 41 (both) Nancy Hogue.

The Georgia Peach
42-43 *The Sporting News;* 44 (left) National Baseball Library, Cooperstown, NY; 44 (right) Library of Congress; 45 (top) National Baseball Library, Cooperstown, NY; 45 (bottom) Ron Menchine Collection/Renée Comet Photography; 46 Pat Quinn, Sports Collectors' Store; 47 National Baseball Library, Cooperstown, NY; 48 Carol Gardner Collection; 49 (top) *Life* Magazine © 1955 Time Inc.; 49 (bottom) AP/Wide World Photos; 50 (left) UPI/Bettmann Newsphotos; 50 (right) Mike Mumby; 51 (both) Ron Menchine Collection;Renée Comet Photography; 53 (left) UPI/Bettmann Newsphotos; 53 (right) Thomas Carwile Collection/Renée Comet Photography; 54 (left) UPI/Bettmann Newsphotos; 54 (right) Brown Brothers; 55 *The Sporting News;* 56 Thomas Carwile Collection/Renée Comet Photography; 57 Mike Mumby.

Cat and Mouse
58-59 Brian Yablonsky; 60 Ron Vesely; 61 Ron Vesely; 62 (left) Thomas Carwile Collection/Renée Comet Photography; 62 (right) Louis Requena; 63 AP/Wide World Photos; 65 Fred Kaplan; 66 Anthony Neste; 67 (top) Louis Requena; 67 (bottom) Dick Raphael; 68 Dick Raphael; 69 (left) Ron Vesely; 69 (right) National Baseball Library, Cooperstown, NY; 70 (left) Malcolm W. Emmons; 70 (right) Bruce L. Schwartzman; 71 Michael Ponzini; 72 (left) National Baseball Library, Cooperstown, NY; 72 (right) AP/Wide World Photos; 73 Walter Iooss, Jr.; 74 John W. McDonough; 75 Bruce L. Schwartzman; 76 Ron Menchine Collection/Renée Comet Photography; 77 Robert Riger; 78 Lee Balterman; 79 Marvin E. Newman.

Little Napoleon and the White Rat
80-81 UPI/Bettmann Newsphotos; 82 (left) The Babe Ruth Museum; 82 (right) Ron Menchine Collection/Renée Comet Photography; 83 Library of Congress; 84 (top) Jerry Wachter/*Sports Illustrated;* 84 (bottom) Bruce L. Schwartzman; 85 National Baseball Library, Cooperstown, NY; 86 Rich Clarkson/*Sports Illustrated;* 87 (top) Lewis Portnoy/Spectra-Action; 87 (bottom) Ron Menchine Collection/Renée Comet Photography; 88 (left) Brown Brothers; 88 (right) Brown Brothers; 89 (left) Brown Brothers; 89 (right) Cleveland Public Library; 90 (left) National Baseball Library, Cooperstown, NY; 90 (right) AP/Wide World Photos; 91 David Walberg; 92 Bruce L. Schwartzman; 93 AP/Wide World Photos; 94 Ronald C. Modra; 95 Ron Vesely.

Don't Look Back
96 Courtesy of Larry Lester; 97 Courtesy of Larry Lester/Renée Comet Photography; 98 (both left) Courtesy of Craig Davidson; 98-99 National Baseball Library, Cooperstown, NY; 100 (both) National Baseball Library, Cooperstown, NY; 101 National Baseball Library, Cooperstown, NY; 102 Ron Menchine Collection/Renée Comet Photography; 103 (both) UPI/Bettmann Newsphotos; 104 National Baseball Library, Cooperstown, NY; 105 National Baseball Library, Cooperstown, NY; 106 (left) Smithsonian Institution; 106 (right) UPI/Bettmann Newsphotos; 107 Robert Riger; 108 Courtesy of Larry Lester; 109 (top) Schomburg Center for Research in Black Culture, New York Public Library; 109 (bottom) National Baseball Library, Cooperstown, NY; 110 National Baseball Library, Cooperstown, NY; 111 (top) National Baseball Library, Cooperstown, NY; 111 (bottom) UPI/Bettmann Newsphotos.

Laying It Down
112-113 Fred Kaplan; 114 Brown Brothers; 115 (left) AP/Wide World Photos; 115 (right) Anthony Neste; 116 (left) National Baseball Library, Cooperstown, NY; 116 (right) Nancy Hogue; 117 AP/Wide World Photos; 118 Ron Menchine Collection/Renée Comet Photography; 119 (top) John D. Hanlon/*Sports Illustrated;* 119 (bottom) Walter Iooss, Jr./*Sports Illustrated;* 120 (left) National Baseball Library, Cooperstown, NY; 120 (right) Bryan Yablonsky; 121 V. J. Lovero/*Sports Illustrated;* 123 Ron Vesely; 124 Ron Menchine Collection/Renée Comet Photography; 125 (left) Anthony Neste; 125 (right) Nancy Hogue; 126 Anthony Neste; 127 (top) Marvin E. Newman; 127 (bottom) UPI/Bettmann Newsphotos.

Center Stage
128 David Walberg; 129 Ron Menchine Collection/Renée Comet Photography; 130 (left) John W. McDonough; 130 (right) AP/Wide World Photos; 131 David Walberg; 132 (left) National Baseball Library, Cooperstown, NY; 132 (right) Otto Greule, Jr./Allsport USA; 133 AP/Wide World Photos; 134 Courtesy of the Texas Rangers; 135 (top) Paul Conklin; 135 (bottom) Courtesy of the Texas Rangers; 136 AP/Wide World Photos; 137 (left) AP/Wide World Photos; 137 (right) Brown Brothers; 138

(left) National Baseball Library, Cooperstown, NY; 138 (right) Bruce L. Schwartzman; 139 Otto Greule, Jr./ Allsport USA; 140 (left) National Baseball Library, Cooperstown, NY; 140 (right) AP/Wide World Photos; 141 (both) UPI/Bettmann Newsphotos; 143 Fred Kaplan; 144 Thomas Carwile Collection/Renée Comet Photography; 145 National Baseball Library, Cooperstown, NY; 146 UPI/Bettmann Newsphotos; 147 Mike Mumby.

The Redbird Express
148-149 UPI/Bettmann Newsphotos; 150 UPI/Bettmann Newsphotos; 151 Ron Menchine Collection/Renée Comet Photography; 152 (left) National Baseball Library, Cooperstown, NY; 152 (right) Brown Brothers; 153 UPI/Bettmann Newsphotos; 154 (left) Ron Menchine Collection/Renée Comet Photography; 154 (right) Brown Brothers; 155(left) UPI/Bettmann Newsphotos; 155 (right) Thomas Carwile Collection/Renée Comet Photography; 156-157 (all) National Baseball Library, Cooperstown, NY; 158 AP/Wide World Photos; 159 UPI/ Bettmann Newsphotos; 160 Estate of Joe York; 161 (top) AP/Wide World Photos; 161 (bottom) Ron Menchine Collection/ Renée Comet Photography; 162 Ron Menchine Collection/Renée Comet Photography; 163 Courtesy of Bill Mead; 164 UPI/Bettmann Newsphotos; 165 (top) Missouri Historical Society; 165 (bottom) UPI/Bettmann Newsphotos.

Steal of the Century
166-167 AP/Wide World Photos; 168 Marvin E. Newman; 169 National Baseball Library, Cooperstown, NY; 170 Lewis Portnoy/Spectra-Action; 171 (top) AP/Wide World Photos; 171 (bottom) Courtesy of © The Topps Company, Inc.; 172 (left) National Baseball Library, Cooperstown, NY; 172 (right) Lewis Portnoy/Spectra-Action; 173 UPI/ Bettmann Newsphotos; 175 National Baseball Library, Cooperstown, NY; 176 Lewis Portnoy/Spectra-Action; 177 (left) Mitchell B. Rebel/Sportschrome East/ West; 177 (right) Lewis Portnoy/ Spectra-Action; 178 Smithsonian Institution; 179 (top) Walter Iooss, Jr./ *Sports Illustrated;* 179 (bottom) UPI/ Bettmann Newsphotos; 180 Marvin E. Newman; 181 Malcolm W. Emmons; 182-183 Ronald C. Modra; 184 Smithsonian Institution; 185 Bill Smith/ *Sports Illustrated.*

ACKNOWLEDGMENTS

The author and editors wish to thank:

Peter P. Clark, Tom Heitz, Bill Deane, Patricia Kelly, Dan Bennett, Sara Kelly, Frank Rollins and the staffs of the National Baseball Hall of Fame and the National Baseball Library, Cooperstown, New York; Nat Andriani, Wide World Photos, New York, New York; Renée Comet, Renée Comet Photography, Washington, D.C.; Joe Borras, Accokeek, Maryland; Dorothy A. Gergel, Springfield, Virginia; Dave Kelly, Library of Congress, Washington, D.C.; Karen Carpenter and Sunny Smith, *Sports Illustrated,* New York, New York; Jim Huffman, Schomburg Center for Research in Black Culture, New York Public Library, New York, New York; John Holway, Alexandria, Virginia; James A. Riley, Cocoa, Florida; Wayne Wilson, Amateur Athletic Foundation, Los Angeles, California; Clarence "Lefty" Blasco, Van Nuys, California; Robert Harding and Ellen Hughes, National Museum of American History, Smithsonian Institution, Washington, D.C.; Helen Bowie Campbell and Gregory J. Schwalenberg, Babe Ruth Museum, Baltimore, Maryland; Dennis Goldstein, Atlanta, Georgia; Stephen P. Gietschier, *The Sporting News;* Wade Cappetta, Nick Cappetta, Curry Printing, Alexandria, Virginia; Kim Briggs, Alexandria, Virginia; Julie Harris, Arlington, Virginia; Jayne E. Rohrich, Alexandria, Virginia.

Illustrations: 30, 86, 135, 142 by Dale Glasgow; 12, 64, 122 by Juan Thomassie; 52, 92, 174 by Sam Ward.

World of Baseball is produced and
published by Redefinition, Inc.

WORLD OF BASEBALL

Editor	Glen B. Ruh
Design Director	Robert Barkin
Production Director	Irv Garfield
Senior Writer	Jonathan Kronstadt
Features Editor	Sharon Cygan
Text Editor	Carol Gardner
Picture Editing	Rebecca Hirsh
	Louis P. Plummer
Design	Edwina Smith
	Sue Pratt
	Collette Conconi
	Monique Strawderman
Copy Preparation	Anthony K. Pordes
	Ginette Gauldfeldt
	Kimberly Fornshill Holmlund
Editorial Research	Janet Pooley
	Mark Lazen
	Ed Dixon
Index	Lynne Hobbs

REDEFINITION

Administration	Margaret M. Higgins
	June M. Nolan
Fulfillment Manager	Karen DeLisser
Marketing Director	Wayne B. Butler
Finance Director	Vaughn A. Meglan
PRESIDENT	Edward Brash

Library of Congress Cataloging-in-Publication Data
Speed/Steve Fiffer.
(World of Baseball)
 1. Baseball—United States—History.
I. Title. II. Series.
GV863.A1F54   1990   90–32315
796.357'0973—dc20
ISBN 0–924588–08–X

CONTRIBUTORS

Steve Fiffer, the author of *Speed,* graduated from
Yale and the University of Chicago Law School.
He has written on baseball for *Sport, Sports
Illustrated, Inside Sports* and *The New York
Times,* and is the author of a book entitled *How
to Watch Baseball.* He learned to bunt in the
fourth grade in an attempt to handle the powerful
fastballs of eighth-grade pitchers.

Henry Staat is Series Consultant for World
of Baseball. A member of the Society for
American Baseball Research since 1982, he
helped initiate the concept for the series. He is
an editor with Wadsworth, Inc., a publisher of
college textbooks.

Ron Menchine, an adviser and sports collector,
shared baseball materials he has been collecting
for 40 years. A radio sportscaster and sports
director, he announced the last three seasons of
the Washington Senators.

The editors also wish to thank the following
writers for their contributions to this book:
Randy Rieland, Washington, D.C.; Robert
Kiener, Washington, D.C.; Gerald Jonas, New
York, NY; Regina Dennis, Alexandria, VA;
Andrew Keegan, Alexandria, VA.

This book is one of a series that celebrates
America's national pastime.

Redefinition also offers World of Baseball Top
Ten Stat Finders.

For subscription information and prices, write:
    Customer Service, Redefinition Inc.
    P.O. Box 25336
    Alexandria, Virginia 22313

The text of this book is set in Century Old
Style; display type is Helvetica and Gill Sans. The
paper is 70 pound Warrenflo Gloss supplied by
Stanford Paper Company. Typesetting by
Intergraphics, Inc., Alexandria, Virginia. Color
separation by Lanman Progressive, Washington,
D.C. Printed and bound by Ringier America, New
Berlin, Wisconsin.